HENRY CLAY

Statesman and Patriot

Henry Clay:

ILLUSTRATED BY CHARLES WALKER

Statesman and Patriot

REGINA Z. KELLY

HOUGHTON MIFFLIN COMPANY

BOSTON   The Riverside Press Cambridge

Contents

Library of Congress Catalog Card No. 60-6697

CHAPTER 1

"Tarleton Is

Coming!"

The Negro boys, Sam and Jim, slowly closed the road gate of Clay's Spring. The last of the horses and carriages were going away after Mr. Clay's funeral.

Then a horseman galloped by. "Tarleton is coming!" he shouted, pointing toward the south.

As fast as they could, the boys ran up the crushed shell pathway to the house. "Tarleton is coming! Tarleton is coming!" they shrieked, their eyes wide with fright.

Mrs. Clay hurried to the front porch. Her children and the house servants were there almost as quickly.

7

"How do you know? Who told you?" Mrs. Clay cried.

"I'll get Pa's gun," offered George, the oldest Clay boy, moving toward the inside of the house.

"No! No! They'll shoot you!" exclaimed his mother.

"What shall we do, Ma?" asked John, the next in age.

"There's no time to do anything." Mrs. Clay hesitated. "Maybe even the British will respect a young widow and her children."

"Is Tarleton bad, Ma?" asked Henry. He was only four years old, and his mother had been holding him close to her side.

"He's a British officer, son. He's been raiding plantations in Virginia," she answered.

"Why?"

"We're at war. We're fighting the British," she explained.

"Don't bother telling him about the Revolution, Ma," said George. "He won't understand."

"I will, too," said Henry, but he held on a

little bit tighter to his mother's hand.

"Let's hide the food," urged John. "Come on, everybody!"

"We're too late," said Mrs. Clay, her face a little pale. "They're coming now."

Over the white picket fence and up the dusty path came a band of mounted soldiers. They were dressed in green coats trimmed with gold, for Tarleton's men did not wear the British red coats. At their head, waving his sword for them to follow, was a handsome young officer in the same uniform, and with a plumed hat.

Mrs. Clay's eyes were fearful. She held out her arms as if to hold all her children, and they and the servants drew close. But George, the oldest child, had an idea. Once more, he moved toward the fireplace over which hung his father's long-barrelled gun.

"No, George! No!" cried his mother.

Yelling wildly and pulling up their horses with plunging leaps, the soldiers were quickly dismounting.

"Search every inch of the house and the

grounds," shouted Tarleton as he jumped from his horse. Already, his men were pushing the family aside and rushing into the house. "Take the horses from the barn, and the food from the cellar and the smokehouse. And see if there's any silver anywhere. Cut the mattresses open. Shake out the feathers."

"Look over there, sir," called a soldier,

pointing to the grave with its freshly turned earth at the end of the garden. "That's where they've hidden the silver."

Mrs. Clay screamed and ran toward Tarleton, tumbling little Henry to the ground.

"That's my husband's grave!" she cried. "Don't you dare touch it."

But the officer pushed her aside. "You'll not play that trick on us," he said sharply. "You heard we were coming and hid the silver. Well, we caught you this time."

There was loud laughter from the soldiers near him.

George put his arm around his mother as she wept. The other children drew near, watching silently, but their eyes were angry. Henry held tightly to Mrs. Clay's hand, and his blue eyes, too, were dark with anger. These men were making his mother cry. They were digging into his father's grave. He hated them.

By this time, two of the soldiers had pushed aside some of the newly turned earth of the grave. They looked surprised and said some-

11

thing to the commander. Those who were near peered into the grave, then stood awkwardly quiet for a few minutes. But Mrs. Clay and her family had moved into the house. There was no further hurt these men could do to them.

For a while, Mrs. Clay sat in her big chair near the open fireplace, with Henry leaning against her shoulder and giving her soft pats on her arm. He was the most loving of her children, she was thinking. The rest were good and helpful, but slow to show their affection. Henry was different. He was her dearest.

The door was opened quickly, and Colonel Tarleton came in with his orderly. "Tell the men to leave everything in the cellar and smokehouse and to go outside," he ordered his aide.

Then the officer turned toward Mrs. Clay. His face was a little red as he spoke. "I'm sorry, ma'am," he said stiffly. "I did not mean to insult the grave of your husband. But we've been fooled before by you rebels."

He walked toward the center of the room and threw a handful of silver coins on the table. "Here's something for your trouble."

Mrs. Clay moved toward the table, her head held proudly, her dark eyes filled with contempt. With a swift movement, she swept the coins into her apron. Then she walked to the fireplace and tossed them on the burning logs.

Warm looks of praise were on the faces of her children.

"You showed him, Ma!" cried George.

Even Henry was smiling. He did not understand the meaning of what his mother had done, yet his heart swelled with pride. But Colonel Tarleton had left the room.

There were shouts of men and the jangling of horses and arms outside. Then all the British soldiers were gone.

"Here's Captain Hal!" exclaimed John, who had been watching from the window. Bright looks of relief were on the faces of everyone.

A few minutes later, a pleasant-faced man was in the room. He was their neighbor, Captain Henry Watkins, the commander of the local militia. His brother was married to Mrs. Clay's sister. Captain Hal, as the children called him, was a favorite with the Clays.

"I rode over here as soon as I heard the news," he said. "But I guess I'm too late. I saw the last of Tarleton's men jump over the fence as I rounded the bend in the road."

"They took some food and a couple of the Negroes," said Mrs. Clay. "I thank you for coming, Captain Watkins."

"They dug into Pa's grave," said George. "I wanted to shoot at them, but Ma wouldn't let me."

"Tarleton gave Ma some money, and she threw it into the fire," added John excitedly.

"Right there on the logs," said Henry, tugging at the visitor's coat. "Look!"

There were partly melted coins scattered on the logs.

"You're a brave woman, Elizabeth," said the Captain.

But to himself he wondered if bravery alone would be enough, now that the British were swarming over Virginia. He knew that the local militia were too few and widely scattered to hold them back. If only General Washington would come to their aid, or that fine young French officer, General Lafayette.

The Captain then went to the cellar and smokehouse with the boys to straighten out

15

the confusion made by the British. But his thoughts were still on Mrs. Clay and her children. She had a good plantation and thirty slaves, but only George was able to do a man's work. The girls were under twelve, and Henry and little Porter were hardly more than babies. *Well, I'll do what I can for them,* thought Captain Watkins.

He stayed for supper and helped with the evening chores. Then they all gathered in front of the fireplace and talked about how they would manage, now that Mr. Clay was dead.

"Our land is wearing out, and our tobacco crop gets smaller each year," said Mrs. Clay.

Captain Watkins nodded. His own farm was not very good. The whole neighborhood was called the "Slashes," because it was filled with deep pockets in the earth from which the water seldom drained.

"I'd like to move out to Kentucky," continued Mrs. Clay. "I've heard the land is so rich out there that it will grow anything."

"My brother John has a farm near Lexington," said Captain Watkins. "He wants me to come out there."

The children then began asking eager questions about Kentucky.

"It's time you young ones went to bed," said their mother, "We've had a long, hard day, and there will be plenty of work to do in the morning."

"Can't Henry say a piece for me first?" asked Captain Watkins.

Mrs. Clay smiled. "He knows a new one. A wounded soldier stopped here last week on his way home from Valley Forge and taught it to him. He said all the soldiers were singing it. Do you remember that piece, Henry?"

But her small son needed no urging. He walked quickly to the center of the room and made a stiff bow with one hand on his chest. "Yankee Doodle," he announced.

Everybody clapped politely.

Captain Watkins clapped loudest of all. Henry was his favorite. *He is like his father,* the Captain was thinking. Besides being a

17

planter, Mr. Clay had been a preacher. Even though there was no regular church, he had conducted prayer meetings and on Sunday had preached to his neighbors. But of all his children, only Henry spoke easily in public. In fact, he liked to speak his "pieces."

He stood up straight and ready now, a little boy with long blond hair tied in a pigtail in the back. He was barelegged and, like his brothers, wore a full-sleeved cotton shirt, and tight breeches of homespun wool. His eyes were merry and bright blue, but he had a crooked nose. His wide mouth made him look like an ugly little imp until he smiled.

Then his face was so bright and full of expression that one never thought of his ugliness.

"Begin, dear," prompted his mother.

> *Yankee Doodle came to town,*
> *Riding on a pony.*
> *Stuck a feather in his hat,*
> *And called it macaroni.*

Henry recited clearly and slowly. Then he made another stiff bow and smiled cheerfully as everyone clapped.

"He's a bright boy," said the Captain to Mrs. Clay, as the children went up the narrow stairs to their attic rooms. "He should get some schooling — and go to Richmond when he's grown."

Mrs. Clay looked a little frightened. "He's so young," she said. "I wouldn't want him to go to Richmond." Then she added, "He can go to the Old Field School under Master Peter Deacon. Henry knows his letters already and can count to ten. He'll get schooling here in Hanover."

Captain Watkins only nodded. *That won't be enough for Henry,* was his thought.

19

CHAPTER 2

A Runaway Slave

Henry was fishing with the two Negro boys, Sam and Jim, in Machump's Creek. This was a favorite spot for the boys, for it was at the foot of the slope on which stood Henry's home, Clay's Spring.

"Your Ma says we had better catch a string of fish by dinnertime, or we'll have to help with the tobacco cutting," said Sam, looking anxiously at his quiet line.

Sam and Jim were about two years older than Henry, who was nine now. The boys, however, frequently played with him, although they were old enough to work in the field. In his will, Henry's father had left Jim and Sam to Henry. Whenever possible, his mother allowed them to be his playmates.

"I'll ask Cap Hal to go fishing with us after

dinner," promised Henry. "I heard him tell Ma that he wasn't going to take the tobacco to Hanover until tomorrow."

"Your step-pa is pretty good to you," said Jim.

Henry nodded. Captain Watkins had married Mrs. Clay about a year after the death of her husband. He was good to all the children, but Henry was still his favorite.

"You've got a bite, Marse Henry," whispered Sam. He pointed to Henry's line which was beginning to twitch.

Each boy held his breath in an effort to be quiet. There were two or three jerks on the line, and Henry's blue eyes grew wide and bright. Then a twig snapped. Henry jumped, and his line suddenly grew slack.

"What did you do that for, Sam?" cried Henry crossly. "My fish got away."

"I didn't do a thing. I haven't even moved," protested Sam.

Jim turned toward the woods in back of them. "That noise came from over there." He was motionless now as he stared almost unbelievingly at the thick grove of trees.

Henry looked at Jim, then turned in the same direction. The color slowly left his cheeks.

Framed in the bushes was the face of a Negro man. His eyes were bloodshot. His black skin was cut and matted with blood and dirt. Big tears were slowly rolling down his cheeks. His great rough hand had stopped just two inches from the heap of corn bread and cold slices of fried bacon which the boys expected to eat for lunch.

Henry saw the slowly moving tears.

"Are you hungry?" he asked. There was no fear in his voice.

The Negro nodded, his eyes sad and begging.

"Go ahead. Eat it," urged Henry.

In a moment, the man had crashed through the bushes and grabbed the corn bread with both hands. For a little while there was no sound except his swallowing of the food.

Henry and the Negro boys watched. Their eyes showed their understanding.

"He's really hungry," said Jim.

But concern was now in Henry's face. "Did you run away?" he asked.

Instantly, the man pushed back into the bushes.

"Don't go," said Henry. "We won't tell. Where did you come from?"

"From Marse Harry Little's place," mumbled the Negro, creeping out again.

"How long have you been in the woods?"

"I don't know. Three — four days. He sold my wife and boy last week. He beat me when I cried."

Mr. Harry Little! Henry had heard his mother and Captain Watkins talking about this man. He had just moved near them and had about twenty slaves. But already people were talking about the way he treated his slaves.

He whipped them. He made them live in tumble-down cabins and gave them hardly enough to eat. He broke up families and sold Negroes whenever he could make any money by doing so.

24

Not one of the Negroes at Clay's Spring had ever felt a whip. They had good cabins and plenty of food. Most of them had their own garden patches. When they did extra work, they were given money by their master or mistress. Some of them had saved enough to buy their freedom. Not even when Mr. Clay had died had any of the Negroes been sold to other masters. Sam and Jim were as dear to Henry as his own brothers.

It isn't right that this poor man should be treated so cruelly, thought Henry.

"We'll help you get away," he said. "What's your name?"

"Dilsey," said the Negro. "I know the way to the river. I can get across to freedom, if nobody catches me first."

"You come back here tonight, Dilsey, when it's dark," said Henry. "I'll bring you some food." He turned to the boys. "We'd better go home now. We've got lots to do."

On the way to the house, Henry planned how they would help Dilsey. Sam and Jim were to tell Sally, the cook, that they had had no dinner, and she would give them the leftovers.

Henry gave them the blue cotton handkerchief from around his neck. "Tie up the food in this and put it under the bush back of the well," he said. "I'll take it to Dilsey."

"Won't you be scared? Going to the woods at night?" asked Sam, frightened at the very thought of the dark, lonely forest.

"Of course not," said Henry. He spoke very loud so the boys wouldn't know how really frightened he was.

At supper that night, the family talked about the news of Dilsey's escape.

"Harry Little ought to lose his slaves," said Captain Watkins. "He treats them like beasts."

"We've always owned slaves, but I'm sure none of them has ever wanted to run away," said Henry's mother.

"I don't like to own slaves, Ma," said Henry with a frown. "Can't I free Sam and Jim?"

"You can if you want to. Remember that

they belong to you," said his mother.

"But it wouldn't be wise to free them until they can earn their own living," said Captain Watkins. "Right now, we can do more for them than they can do for themselves."

Henry lingered in front of the fire long after the rest of the family had gone to the loft rooms upstairs. Finally his mother said he must go to bed.

"I have to fill the wood box for Sally first," said Henry. It was his special chore to keep the kitchen supplied with fuel.

"There was plenty of wood by the fire after supper," said Mrs. Watkins. "You can wait."

"Sally wants to bake bread the first thing in the morning," said Henry. He crossed his fingers behind his back and hoped the Lord would forgive him for telling such a big fib. But telling a fib couldn't be as bad as letting poor Dilsey go hungry.

The handkerchief filled with food was under the bush. From there, Henry ran down the hillside, which was bright with moonlight. He waited at the edge of the creek. But only the sound of croaking frogs and the murmur of insects could be heard.

"Dilsey!" he called softly. Then again — "Dilsey!"

"I'm — I'm here," Dilsey's voice was shaky.

The black bulk of the Negro came out of the deep shadows. In a few minutes he was gulping down the food.

"I'll be back tomorrow night at this same place," promised Henry. "I'll bring you some more food and some clothes. Maybe you can get to the river then."

All the next day, the three boys did what they could to store up food. In a household like Henry's, where supplies were plentiful and there were many mouths to feed, a little food would not be missed. By evening there were two fat bundles under the bushes at the well.

That evening Henry could think of no excuse to delay his bedtime. During the day, he had found two cotton shirts and a pair of breeches that had belonged to his father in a deerskin trunk in the storeroom. He had hidden them under the bed in the loft room he shared with his brother Porter.

After they had gone to bed, Henry listened until he was sure Porter was sound asleep. Careful not to make any noise, Henry slipped from the bed and pulled his breeches over his shirt. Then he took the bundle of clothes from under the bed and dropped it out of the window to the ground.

Inch by inch, Henry slid out of the window and down the steep roof of the house. A branch of an apple tree touched the roof, and with a swing Henry was on this and in a minute had jumped to the ground.

The moon was just as bright tonight. The sounds of frogs and insects were all that could be heard. Carefully Henry moved in the shadows toward the well. He knelt and knotted the handkerchiefs filled with food and slipped them under his arm.

As he rose, he heard the baying of a hound. Then another — and another. There were distant cries.

Suddenly, the sound of a shot crackled in the air. The wild clamor of the hounds filled the night. Another shot came sharp and clear. Then there was only the yelping of the hounds and sharp calls of command.

With his heart thick in his throat, Henry waited, crouching on his knees. Candles were being lighted in the house. He saw his brothers and sisters looking out of the windows and calling back and forth. Some of the Negroes came running from the cabins. Henry crept toward the house, still keeping in the shadows.

There was the pounding and galloping of horses and the barking of hounds drawing near the house now. The front door opened, and Henry's mother and his stepfather stood in the flood of light.

The two men on horseback and a pack of dogs came up the shell pathway. As they pulled up in front of the house, Henry recognized the first man. He was John Lawrence, the sheriff of Hanover County.

"I thought I'd stop and tell you we've shot a Negro in the woods," called the sheriff to Captain Watkins. "He's a runaway slave from Mr. Little's place."

"Is he badly hurt?" asked Mrs. Watkins. "If he is, you had better bring him here."

"I guess he's dead, ma'am," said the sheriff. "I wanted to shoot him in the leg, but I missed my aim."

"Poor, poor man," said Mrs. Watkins.

"Yes, ma'am. Mr. Little will be hopping mad at losing his man," said the sheriff.

"I meant the Negro," said Mrs. Watkins, and closed the door.

The lights in the house went out. The windows were closed. But Henry stayed outside, his face washed with tears as he thought of poor Dilsey.

"If only I could have got to him earlier, he might have escaped," said Henry, half aloud.

Slowly, he went into the house and climbed the dark staircase. There was no need for keeping things secret now.

"As soon as Sam and Jim are old enough, I'll tell Cap Hal to set them free," he murmured, as he pulled up the sheet.

"What did you say?" asked Porter sleepily.

"Just something I plan to do," answered Henry.

CHAPTER 3

"Give Me Liberty..."

The schoolroom of the Old Field School in Hanover was sleepily quiet. It was the last day of the term, for it was spring and the children were needed to help in the fields.

The school was a one-room log cabin with a planked floor and a wide fireplace. It was bright today, for the weather was warm and the windows were open. In winter the room was quite dark, for there was only greased paper in the windows to let in the light. The flickering flames of the big fireplace or the single candle on the master's high desk was the only other light.

There were about thirty children in the room, ranging in age from six to thirteen. Henry, who was thirteen, sat with the older children on long, backless benches in front of a sloping shelf built along the walls on three sides of the room. The little ones were seated in the center on long benches. These benches were made of logs cut in half with the rounded side down and raised some distance from the floor by thick wooden pegs.

"We'll have our spelling lesson first," said the teacher, Master Peter Deacon, when the morning prayer had been said. "Now, everyone, sit up straight and fold your hands."

The older children turned around to face him, and waited quietly. But some of the very little ones in the center of the room moved restlessly. Their legs swung from the high benches, and their backs were tired. However, a flick of the bunch of worn switches, which hung near the master's desk, soon ended all disorder.

Master Deacon opened his spelling book. "Spell *sassafras*, Henry Clay," he said.

36

Henry rose. He was glad to stretch his long legs.

"S-a-s-s-a-f-r-a-s," he answered easily.

"Now, everyone," said Master Deacon.

"S-a-s-s-a-f-r-a-s," shouted all the pupils together, while the master beat time with his ruler.

"Spell *geography*, Sarah King," the master said next.

And so the spelling lesson went on, until the list for the day was ended.

"Now I will hear the little ones say their reading. You big boys and girls can do your sums or study from your spelling books."

One by one, the youngest children came up to the master's desk, and he heard their lessons. There were all grades in the room, as well as all ages. The first graders used a hornbook to learn their letters. Henry, like all the older pupils, had a worn copy of Dilworth's Speller. It was a reader and speller combined, with black and white pictures. His older brothers and sisters had used it before

A hornbook

him. It would serve for the younger children when he finished school.

These were the only books in the schoolroom. The pupils learned a little geography from the battered globe on Master Deacon's desk. He taught them history by telling them stories of Virginia before the Revolution. He taught them their tables, and how to add, multiply, subtract, and divide "from his head." The people of Hanover thought Master Deacon was "a fine arithmeticker." He had a "sum book" with the problems he had worked out when he went to school. Each boy and girl in his classroom would also make a sum book.

At last, it was time for recess. For a half hour the children played. Then they came back noisily into the room.

"Now you will write on your slates or in your copybook," said Master Deacon.

The older pupils had copybooks and wrote in ink. Their pens were made from goose quills. Master Deacon kept them sharpened to a fine point with his penknife. The ink was in a horn cup and had been made at home by boiling down the roots of swamp maple. The copybooks were sheets of coarse brown paper sewn together to make a book. They had rough cardboard covers. The pupils themselves had ruled the lines on the paper.

Up and down the rows went the teacher. At the top of each book or slate he wrote in a large, round hand, "Contentment is a virtue." The room was quiet except for the scratching of pens or the squeaking of slate pencils, as each child wrote the sentence over and over again.

Henry was the only one who did not write the sentence in his copybook. This was the last day he was to go to school. Although the school term was seldom more than twelve weeks long, this was his third term with Master Deacon. That was as long as most boys attended school.

There was something Henry wished to finish today, and as Henry had the best penmanship in the class, Master Deacon had given him permission. Henry was copying one of Patrick Henry's famous speeches in his copybook. As he stopped to sharpen his quill with his own penknife, Master Deacon looked over his shoulder.

"You have fine, neat handwriting," said the master. "I am proud of your work."

Henry smiled his thanks. He liked to keep his copybook neat and clean, and he wrote with firm, clear lines.

The teacher looked at the writing of the other pupils, then went to his desk.

"Since this is the last day of school," said Master Deacon, "I shall tell you a history story. After that, Henry will recite a piece."

The boys and girls quickly straightened on their benches. There were pleased looks everywhere.

"How many of you have heard about Patrick Henry?" asked the master with a smile. He knew what the answer would be.

Up went all the hands. Everyone in Hanover County knew about Patrick Henry. His wife's father owned the inn across the road from the courthouse. Patrick Henry had

41

worked in that inn before he became a noted lawyer. His first great speech had been made in that same courthouse. The people had carried him out on their shoulders when it was over.

"I am going to tell you about the speech I heard him make in Richmond before the Revolution," said the master. "The burgesses were meeting in St. John's Church then."

"Why?" asked a boy.

"Because they had fled from the capital at Williamsburg, and St. John's was the largest building in Richmond."

"What's a burgess?" asked another boy.

"One of our lawmakers. The burgesses meet in Richmond now, in the Assembly."

"Was Patrick Henry a burgess?"

"He was. And so was George Washington, and Thomas Jefferson, and Peyton Randolph. They were all there, sitting in those big high-backed pews in St. John's Church."

Master Deacon paused and looked down at his desk.

"Why did Patrick Henry make a speech?" asked Henry, reminding the teacher. Henry knew what had happened, but the rest of the pupils would like to hear.

"Patrick Henry made the speech because he wanted the burgesses to vote for a sum of money to pay for an army and weapons to fight the British," said the master, smiling at Henry. "Some of the burgesses were afraid that this might start war."

"Did they vote the money?" was the next eager question.

"I'll tell you what happened," said the master. "I was in the crowd of people in the graveyard outside the church that day. I could see everything that happened through the church window."

He told them how Patrick Henry had stood up with his wrists held close together as if he were chained like a slave. "He was always a great actor," explained the teacher.

Then he continued, "His voice rang out like a strong bell, and his eyes were like fire. The walls seemed to shake when he spoke. But when he finished, the burgesses voted for what he asked."

"What did he say? What did he say?"

"Be quiet, everybody," said Master Deacon. "Henry will give you his speech."

Henry stepped up to the platform. He had heard the story many times and had learned the speech by heart. In his mind now, he saw Patrick Henry as Master Deacon had described him.

With a move toward the front of the platform, Henry lifted his long, bony hands as if they were chained together. His keen blue eyes were serious. In full, clear tones he repeated Patrick Henry's famous speech.

"Is life so dear, or peace so sweet," he cried out at the end, "as to be purchased at the price of chains and slavery?" Once more Henry raised his close-held hands, so that all the class could imagine they were chained. "I know not what course others may take; but as for me, give me liberty or give me death!"

There was loud applause from the class as Henry bowed. There was nothing they liked

better than to hear Henry Clay make a speech. They thought he was just as good as Patrick Henry — maybe a lot better.

"And that was how Patrick Henry put courage into the hearts of all the burgesses," said the master. "Now, you may all go home. And be civil to anyone you meet."

Henry lingered after the rest. Master Deacon had always taken special interest in him and had taught him Patrick Henry's most famous speeches.

The schoolmaster got part of his pay by boarding around in the homes of his pupils. The time for each household depended on how many children the family had in school. As the Clay family was large, the master spent several weeks each school term at Clay's Spring.

"Will your family be going to Kentucky soon?" asked Master Deacon as he straightened the copybooks.

"They expect to leave in a month."

Ever since Henry's mother had married Captain Watkins, his brother John Watkins had been writing from Lexington and urging them to come to Kentucky. Now they had decided to leave in the late spring, so that they would cross the mountains and be in Kentucky before the cold weather began.

"Are you going with them?" asked the master.

Henry hesitated. "I want to go. But I'd like to be a lawyer — like Patrick Henry."

"And you could be," said the master, "if you'd get a chance to study with some lawyer."

"That's why I'd like to go to Richmond. But I can't go there if we go to Kentucky."

"There must be lawyers in Kentucky," said the master.

"But they're not like the 'bigwigs' of Richmond. All the best lawyers in Virginia are there."

"I suppose you are right," said the master. "Anyhow, I have a present for you. I am going to give you all the speeches of Patrick Henry that I remembered and have copied. At least you can study those in Kentucky."

Carefully, Henry put the neatly written pages in the pocket of his breeches. This was the finest gift the master could give him.

If only I could be a lawyer, thought Henry as he walked the two miles toward home. But how could that be? Of course, the lawyers who were rich and great went to the College of William and Mary. But there were plenty who studied by clerking in some lawyer's office. Patrick Henry had studied by himself. There were folks who said he didn't know much about law. Yet he always won his cases.

Henry stopped. "Gentlemen of the jury," he said aloud, for there was no one around. Then he frowned. There was more to being a lawyer than making speeches. But making

47

speeches was the part about law that Henry liked best. He never had liked to study very much.

When he came home, the older boys and his mother and Captain Watkins were studying a map of the Cumberland Gap.

"You're late, Henry," said his mother. "The rest of the children have been home an hour from school."

"You had better feed the pigs," said Captain Watkins. "I can hear them grunting from here."

Henry took the basket of corn out to the pigs, and soon the grunts grew less noisy. From his pocket he took a copy of one of Patrick Henry's speeches, which Master Deacon had given him, and glanced at it once more.

"As for me, give me liberty or give me death!" he shouted.

There was a loud clapping of hands.

Henry turned. His stepfather was grinning at him.

"What are you trying to do?" asked Captain Watkins. "Make the pigs vote for you?"

"At least, they won't clap for me and vote for someone else," laughed Henry.

"You're a great speech maker, Henry," said his stepfather. "I've thought that ever since you were a little boy. You're as good as Patrick Henry."

Henry's face glowed. "Do you really think so?"

"Better, I'd say."

"Oh! You're making fun of me."

"No, I'm not. That's why I've done something to help you get to Richmond."

Henry looked surprised. "I didn't think you knew I wanted to go."

"Your ma and I have known it for a long time. So I asked Colonel Tinsley to get you a clerkship with his brother, Mr. Peter Tinsley, in the office of the Chancery Court. He's the clerk there."

"Can I be a clerk right away?" asked Henry eagerly.

"Colonel Tinsley said there might not be an opening right now. But in the meantime, you can work in Richard Denny's store in Richmond. He will be happy to have you."

"What's the Chancery Court?" asked Henry.

"It's the court where cases about property are tried. Colonel Tinsley told me that. He said lots of important people and lawyers go there," said Captain Watkins.

Important lawyers! Even Patrick Henry might appear in the Chancery Court for a case. Henry was so delighted, he could hardly talk.

"When do I go?" he asked.

"In a few days. Colonel Tinsley will take you to Richmond."

Suddenly, Henry was frightened. In a few days! It was all happening so fast. The others would be leaving for Kentucky soon. He might not see them for a long time — maybe never.

Captain Watkins must have guessed how he felt.

"Go in to your ma," he said gently. "She's made you a new homespun suit to wear. She'll want you to try it on."

CHAPTER 4

A Young Storekeeper

Henry opened wide the heavy wooden shutters on the window of Mr. Denny's shop on Brick Row in Richmond. He had swept the floor. Now he must sweep the brick sidewalk in front of the shop.

"You have made a nice display for me," said Mr. Denny, coming to the door of the shop.

They both gazed proudly through the small-paned window. New spring bonnets, cut-glass bottles of perfume, boxes of Spanish cigars, bottles of rum and brandy, brightly colored playing cards, and partly opened rolls of silk, velvet, and calico were crowded on the shelves.

"My new shipment of goods from London came just in time for the meeting of the Assembly," said Mr. Denny. "After breakfast, you must go to the print shop and get extra copies of our advertisement. You can give them to people in the Market Square on your way back."

It was still early in the morning when Henry walked to the print shop, but already the town was ready for business. Carriages rattled along the rutted streets, with women and children riding in most of them. The men rode on horseback, for a Virginian would mount his horse to cross the street to buy a package of snuff.

There were all kinds of shops along the way. Most of them were built even with the sidewalk and had little gardens closed in by picket fences on the side. The shops were on the ground floor, and the shopkeepers and their families lived in the dormer-windowed rooms above.

None of the shops was numbered, but most of them had signs to show what was sold.

54

There was a mortar and pestle in front of the chemist's. The barber had wig stands and false heads in his window. But there was a red and white striped pole outside. The barber was the surgeon-dentist as well, and the red and white pole showed his skill in making bandages.

The shoemaker had a tall pair of boots on his sign. The milliner's showed a woman's fine bonnet. The tailor had a pair of scissors and a spool of thread. The finest display was in the window of the silversmith. Drinking cups, candle holders, tea pots, and sugar bowls glittered in the morning sun.

In the window of the print shop, there were all kinds of advertisements. Henry entered and got a handful of the one telling about Mr. Denny's sale.

Henry stayed for a while in the print shop, for all the news of Richmond buzzed through its open doors. The *Gazette,* which was the weekly newspaper, was published here. Even the smell of the ink for the press was exciting for Henry. Usually, the printer had time for a chat with Henry, who was always interested in people and what was happening to them.

But the printer was busy with his apprentice this morning. "Now mind your p's and q's," he was telling the boy as Henry picked up his papers. "And don't get them mixed. Remember, they both have long tails."

Henry walked slowly back to the shop. He stopped at the Market Square to give shoppers the advertisements and answer questions about prices.

But he was disappointed that he had heard no news in the print shop of the Assembly meeting. He had been in Richmond over six months. So far he had not even seen one of the great lawmakers, much less heard the speeches they made in the Capitol building.

I'll never become a lawyer, thought Henry sadly.

He was homesick, too, for his family. "I wish I had gone to Kentucky with Ma," he sighed.

A carriage load of ladies was in front of Denny's shop by the time Henry returned.

"Hurry!" Mr. Denny called to him. "I need you to keep a record of the sales for the day."

Into the big leatherbound book, Henry neatly wrote each sale as it was made. He also helped behind the counter.

Once when Henry came back from carrying a big pile of packages to a carriage, Mr. Denny patted him on the back. "I think that lady made extra purchases because you were so polite to her," said the shopkeeper.

Henry grinned with pleasure. He had made a special effort to bow and smile and serve people as well as he could. He enjoyed helping people and being polite to them.

"Here comes Mr. Nelson and his family," he said, as a carriage with two fine horses stopped at the hitching post. "I know they'll buy a lot."

Mr. Nelson was a wealthy planter who lived near Yorktown. Each year his whole family came to Richmond when the Assembly was in session. By the time he had finished his shopping, even Mr. Denny had to help carry the bundles to the carriage.

Then Mr. Nelson came back to the shop to pay his bill. He dumped the contents of a leather bag of coins on the counter. There were English, Spanish, Dutch, and French coins. Some of them were worn, and others had edges which seemed shaved a little.

From one of his pockets, Mr. Nelson pulled out a bundle of slips of paper. They were warehouse receipts for the tobacco and cotton he had stored in Richmond. So far, no paper money was printed by the government.

By this time, a half dozen new shoppers had come in.

"You count up what Mr. Nelson owes us, Henry," said Mr. Denny. "Then figure out what his money is worth in United States dollars."

"Can this boy count that well?" asked Mr. Nelson, looking surprised.

"He is very quick at figures," said Mr. Denny. "But I'll check your bill when he has finished."

Henry's cheeks were warm with pride at what Mr. Denny had said. Carefully, he totaled the amount. Then he figured out in United States dollars the value of the different kinds of money Mr. Nelson had given him. Henry was used to doing this. Although the United States now minted coins, there were few around. Most of the people used the various foreign coins that were still in the country.

Mr. Nelson had fifty cents in change coming to him. So Henry took one of the silver dollars to Jim, the Negro in charge of the money-chopping block. With a sure stroke of his sharp axe, Jim cut the dollar into four equal parts. Two were given to Mr. Nelson. None of the small United States coins were in general use yet, so dollars were cut into "bits" for change. People called these "cut silver" and kept the bits in little money bags.

As soon as Mr. Denny was free, he checked Henry's figures and found them to be correct.

"I hope the time will come when we have just one kind of money to carry on trade," said Mr. Denny to his customer.

"And a good banking system like that of England and France," added Mr. Nelson.

Henry said nothing, but he was paying close attention. For the first time, he realized that trading meant more than just exchanging goods for money. Trading could bring

all the people of the country together and make them into a real united nation. But we would have to have good roads and the same kind of money, or we would be trading just like the Indians. He wondered if the lawmakers up on the hill knew this and were making the right kind of laws.

It was long after supper, and Mr. Denny and Henry had lighted candles on the high-topped desk in the shop before they were finished with their work for the day. Henry had copied so many items in the big journal, that he had had to sharpen his quill pen three times.

Mr. Denny was greatly pleased. He opened his strong box and took out a silver dollar. "I am going to give you this as extra pay for all that you have done," he said.

Then he gazed at the long rows of figures in the book. "I have never had a clerk who wrote as neatly or as carefully."

Just then the bell on the door of the shop jangled, and Colonel Tinsley came into the shop.

"I saw the candles burning, so I thought I would stop for a moment," he said.

"We've made our totals for the day," said Mr. Denny. "But if there's something you need, we could add the amount."

"My purchase can wait," said Colonel Tinsley. "But I have a piece of news that Henry will want to hear."

"Is it anything about my folks?"

"No. About yourself. My brother has a place for you in the Chancery Court. You may start tomorrow, if you wish."

"Tomorrow!" Henry was delighted.

But Mr. Denny shook his head and smiled. "The best clerk I have ever had. Well, your penmanship will do you more good as a clerk in the Chancery Office than here."

CHAPTER 5

At the

Chancery Court

At the top of Shockoe Hill, the white pillars of the new Capitol building in Richmond gleamed in the morning sunshine. Henry walked slowly up the slope. He was wearing the homespun suit with the pepper-and-salt pattern that his mother had made for him, and a ruffled linen shirt stiff with starch. Betty, Mr. Denny's cook, had washed and ironed it for him.

Henry stopped a short distance from the Capitol. Early comers were already going up the steps. Somehow, his eager desire of yesterday had passed away. Whom would he meet in the Chancery Court? How would he be treated? What would be his new tasks?

Faintly in the distance, he caught the

sparkle of sunshine on the brown waters of the James River. Yesterday, he had walked along its banks. Tall, square-masted ships had been moored there. Negroes had been rolling great hogsheads of tobacco and other produce up the gangways of the ships. Mule-drawn carts and covered wagons had rumbled over the bridge that crossed the river.

There had been a smell of hemp, and pine, and tar in the air — and strongest of all, the sour, sweet smell of tobacco. These were the sights, and sounds, and smells that Henry had known yesterday. What would his new life be? Once more, he looked up at the Capitol.

"It's a fine building, isn't it, young man?"

A short, elderly man with a high forehead and long beaked nose was speaking to Henry. The man was well-dressed in plain dark gray, with old-fashioned knee length breeches and buckled shoes.

"Yes, sir," answered Henry politely. *This must be one of the Richmond "bigwigs,"* he thought.

"Thomas Jefferson copied the design from a building he admired in France," said the man. "Well, I must be going. Perhaps I shall see you in Court."

He lifted his broad hat, and Henry saw the old man's bald head with its fringe of curling gray hair. Henry did his best to imitate the man's courteous bow.

He was as polite as if I were someone important, thought Henry.

The meeting gave him courage. With a brisk air, he mounted the flight of steps at the side and entered the rotunda of the Capitol. A Negro porter showed Henry the stairway which led to the basement room of the Chancery Court.

In a few moments, he opened the door of the room, then waited for a moment. The room was dark, and there were candles burning on a long, high-topped desk along the wall. Ten or a dozen clerks were seated on tall stools in front of the desk. Most of them seemed only a few years older than Henry himself.

One of the boys turned as Henry closed the

door and moved into the light. The boy pointed at him and laughed.

"Look at the blackbird that's come to see us," cried the boy. "All he needs is a beak."

Henry flushed. The tails of his homemade pepper-and-salt suit were sticking out behind. His wide mouth was probably like that of a bird. His anger fled, and he grinned at the thought.

"If I were a bird, I'd be looking for a worm in a wooden head," he answered.

There was a roar of laughter from the other boys.

"That serves you right, Will Sharp," they cried.

"You win, fellow," said Will Sharp. He slipped from his stool and came toward Henry with his hand outstretched.

But another boy had moved forward more quickly. He also held out his hand.

"You must be Henry Clay," he said. "Mr. Tinsley told me you were coming. I'm Tom Williamson, the chief clerk here." He turned to the other boy. "And this is William Sharp."

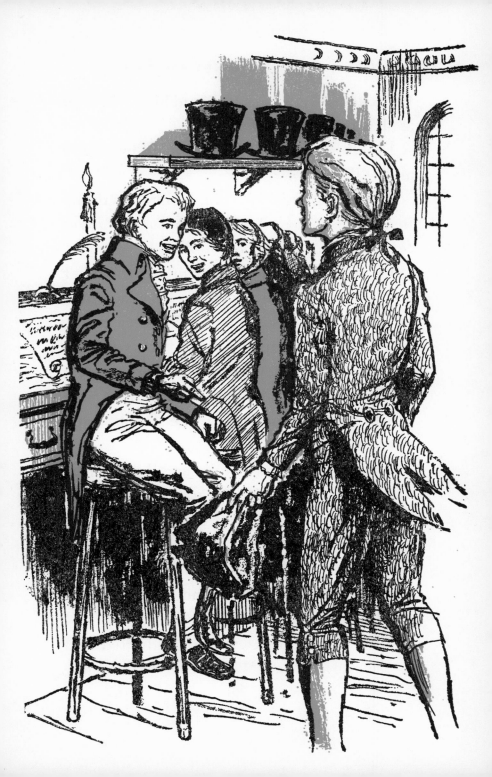

He poked at Will. "Don't mind him. He's not as sharp as his tongue."

Everybody laughed again, including Henry and Will Sharp.

I am going to like it here, Henry was thinking. *These boys don't mind a joke about themselves. And neither do I.*

In a few minutes, Henry had met the other boys. Then he was shown to his place next to Tom Williamson's and told what to do. The boys were copying legal papers for the court. Mr. Tinsley came in later to greet Henry and give him more instructions. He was to have his meals with the Tinsleys and sleep at their house.

There was pleasant talk and laughter as the boys worked. Henry soon felt at ease. But throughout the day, he glanced at the way his comrades were dressed and then at his own garments. Already, his homemade suit was too small for him, and his bony wrists stuck out of the too short sleeves.

Most of the clerks were well-dressed and in the new style. Their coats were close fitting at the waist and had high collars and wide lapels. Their breeches were long and tight, and held by straps under their boots. Most of them had high silk hats with curling brims on the shelf above the long desk.

All the money Mr. Denny had paid Henry was now in his pocket. This evening, he decided, he would order a fine coat and a pair of long, tight-fitting breeches from the tailor on Brick Row.

About a year after Henry had begun clerking in the Chancery Court, the little man whom he had met on the first day came into the basement room. Henry knew him now. He was Mr. George Wythe, one of the most learned and famous lawyers in Virginia. He had signed the Declaration of Independence, had been a member of the Constitutional Convention, and had been the first professor of law at William and Mary.

But most important of all for Henry was the fact the Mr. Wythe was the Chancellor of Virginia. This meant that he was the highest judge in the Chancery Court. Henry had seen him only at a distance since their first meeting. But he always remembered how kind and polite Mr. Wythe had been to him.

As soon as the Chancellor came into the room, Tom Williamson moved forward to greet him.

"What can I do for you, sir?" he asked.

"May I look at the papers your young men are writing?" asked the visitor.

"We will be pleased to have you look at the papers," answered Tom, "for you will see our best penmanship. We are copying these for Mr. Tinsley."

The old man stopped at each clerk's place at the high desk and carefully inspected his written pages. Sometimes, Mr. Wythe's long beaked nose almost touched the desk as he checked. He paused a long time at Henry's place, then went on. But after he reached the end of the line, he came back to Henry.

"I remember you now," he said. "I talked to you one morning on my way to the Court."

"That was my first day here," said Henry.

"And do you like the work?"

"Very much."

"Does it keep you busy?"

"Yes, sir, but I have some time to spare."

"Then, perhaps, you would work for me an hour or so each day." Mr. Wythe held out his hands which were swollen and knotted. "I find it difficult to write now, so I need a secretary."

"It will be a pleasure, sir, to work for you."

Henry had jumped off his stool the moment Mr. Wythe had come back to speak to him. He bowed now as he answered. Somehow, just speaking to this old man made one want to be more polite.

"Then come this afternoon at three," said Mr. Wythe also bowing. "I live on Grace Street. You will find the house easily. There is a large tulip tree in the garden."

CHAPTER 6

Secretary to
Chancellor Wythe

That afternoon, Henry walked west on Shockoe Hill to Mr. Wythe's house near the Capitol. The Chancellor was in his library. Henry had never seen so many books in one room. They filled the shelves all around the room, and more books were piled on the desk and tables.

A servant brought in a tray with a pitcher of strawberry shrub and a plate of small cakes.

"The boys I knew at William and Mary were always hungry," said Mr. Wythe with a smile. "Take all you want."

For two hours after that, he dictated to Henry, though he paused several times to give his young secretary a rest. When the sun was slanting, they stopped.

"I have never seen so many books," said Henry as he was leaving.

"I'll lend you all you care to read," said Mr. Wythe. He picked out several books from a shelf. They were histories and biographies.

A few days later, Henry returned the books. He had found them interesting but had read them quickly.

Mr. Wythe shook his head. "Don't skim when you read, my boy. You should read deeply."

Henry looked around the room. How could he read all those books deeply? How could he read them at all?

Mr. Wythe must have understood his look. "You have your whole life before you," he said with a smile. "Don't ever skim when you read."

Henry was Mr. Wythe's secretary for five years. During that time, he continued as a clerk at the Chancery Court. His fellow clerks were still his good friends. He joined the Debating Club and soon was its best speaker. With Tom Williamson and William Sharp, he went to the meetings of the Assembly and heard the "bigwigs" of Virginia debate.

Once, Patrick Henry was to speak in the Hall of Delegates in the Capitol. Henry and Tom Williamson came early and got seats in the front of the gallery. Long before the trial started every seat was taken, and there were crowds peering through the windows and doorways.

Henry and Tom could hardly wait for the opening of the trial. Neither of them had ever heard Patrick Henry plead a case. On the bench sat Chief Justice Jay with the other judges, all wearing black robes and long white wigs. At a table before them were the lawyers in the case.

The boys leaned forward so that they could get a good look at Patrick Henry. He wore a black woolen suit, old-fashioned in style with short knee breeches. A three-cornered black hat was on the table before him. The only bright note in his dress was the great red cloak thrown over the back of his chair.

But the face and pose of Patrick Henry were even more dismal than his clothes. His head and shoulders were wrapped in heavy woolen mufflers, though the day was warm. He sat with head bowed and eyes half-closed. Once in a while, he fingered a thick, worn notebook.

"They say he has been studying this case for weeks," whispered Tom.

"He's tired out from all that work," said Henry sadly. "He'll never make a speech today."

The case was opened, and at last it was time for Patrick Henry to speak. Almost instantly all the buzzing sounds in the room came to an end.

He rose slowly. He was tall and lean, though his shoulders were stooped. His skin looked wrinkled and pale, and his blue eyes were still half-closed.

Henry and Tom nudged each other and shook their heads. This was the end of their great lion-like hero.

"It is a hardship," began Patrick Henry in a low voice, "to put the oar into the hands of an old man with one foot in the grave, who was weak even in his best days, and far inferior to the able men with him."

He bowed courteously to the judges before him.

The lawyers who were opposed to him smiled a little.

"They think they've won the case already," said Tom angrily.

"He's not quite sixty years," whispered Henry. "Why does he speak like an old man?"

"Ssssh!" said those around him.

Tom poked Henry excitedly. "Look!" he said.

Patrick Henry had finished with his opening statements. He was standing erect now. His skin was smooth and warm with color. His blue eyes were wide and sparkling. His voice pealed out like a trumpet.

For more than an hour, he spoke. There was not another sound in the room. The color grew so hot in Henry Clay's cheeks,

he thought the blood would burst in his face. Shivers ran up and down his back.

This was like the stories Henry had heard. Here was Patrick Henry, the great play actor. He was pretending to be helpless, then sweeping everything before him. Here was the man who, with the music and the passion in his voice, could make men follow him like the Pied Piper.

At last, the speech was over. A few days later the case was ended, and Patrick Henry had won. He had made a speech that Henry Clay was never to forget.

The five years that Henry spent as secretary to Mr. Wythe made a great change in the boy who was a clerk in the Chancery Court. He learned something of the law behind the decisions that were made in the Court. He became familiar with the legal phrases that were used in the papers that he copied for Mr. Tinsley.

From the letters Henry copied for Mr. Wythe and the long friendly talks he had with the old man, Henry not only learned law but gained other knowledge. He still skimmed through the books that the Chancellor loaned him, but he remembered much of what he read.

There was more, however, that Henry learned than the knowledge that came from books and conversation. Almost without knowing it, he began to copy the courtly manners and the gentle courtesy of Mr. Wythe. He also understood and shared some of the principles in which the Chancellor believed and which he practiced.

Henry learned something, too, from the great men who came to see the Chancellor. Thomas Jefferson, James Madison, John Marshall, James Monroe, Benjamin Harrison, and certain of the lawyers whom Mr. Wythe had taught at William and Mary often visited the Chancellor. Of them all, Henry liked and admired Jefferson the most.

When Jefferson was in Richmond, the tall, red-haired statesman called on Mr. Wythe. Henry knew that after graduating from William and Mary, Jefferson had studied law with Mr. Wythe for five years. He had been like a foster son to the old man.

Mr. Wythe is just as interested in me, thought Henry gratefully. His eyes grew bright as he realized what that might mean to him in the future.

Then he remembered that Jefferson had been a good student and constant reader. Henry felt uncomfortable as he thought how he had "skimmed" through the books he had read. *I'll study every book Mr. Wythe gives me from now on,* Henry determined. Yet in a few weeks, he had forgotten the promise he had made to himself.

But he was happy when he was invited to remain during Jefferson's visits with the Chancellor. He nearly burst with pride at being included as an equal in the talks of the two men.

"Come visit me at Monticello," Jefferson urged Henry. "I'll show you my library and all my inventions."

One day, when Henry was nearly twenty, Mr. Wythe and Henry talked about what

Henry planned to do with his future.

"Now that you are nearly of age," asked the Chancellor, "how do you expect to earn your living?"

"I want to be a lawyer, sir," said Henry. "I'd like to plead cases like Patrick Henry."

"I thought that," said Mr. Wythe. "And so I have secured a clerkship for you with our Attorney General, Robert Brooke."

Henry was delighted. Robert Brooke was one of the best lawyers in Virginia, and had been governor for two years.

"Where shall I live if I give up my clerkship at the Chancery?" asked Henry.

"Mr. Brooke says he will be happy to have you live in his own home."

The Chancellor smiled. He had seen the change in Henry through the years. Henry was over six feet tall now. He dressed well because he liked fine clothes. His yellow hair was cut short in the new fashion, but his features were as homely as ever. However, when he smiled, his whole face lighted up, and he was a handsome and likable fellow.

No longer was he awkward as in his first days at the Capitol. His manners were charming, and he was a favorite with everybody.

In a short time, Henry went to live in Mr. Brooke's fine, white-pillared house near the Capitol. Mrs. Brooke's youngest brother, Tom Ritchie, lived with them, and so Henry had companionship of his own age. He was welcomed in the homes of Tom's friends and joined in all their fun and sport. He rode in the fox hunts, attended the racing meets, and went to the Assembly balls.

Henry wore short satin breeches, silk stockings, and buckled shoes for these dances, for this was still the costume worn at formal parties in Virginia. He danced the minuet now, as well as reels and square dances. With his grace of manner, and the ease with which he talked, Henry won the liking of young and old.

"Oh, Mamma!" said the pretty girls of Richmond. "Mr. Clay dances so wonderfully and makes such fine speeches."

But the mothers, although they liked Henry, smiled and shook their heads. He was only

a clerk in the law office, and he did not have a penny to his name. Their daughters must make better matches.

Henry's days with Mr. Brooke were not all fun. He worked hard and studied the practical part of law. He went to court with Mr. Brooke and found out how cases were conducted. He listened to Mr. Brooke talk with his clients. He copied endless legal papers. He read the books in the attorney's library. In this way, Henry learned more of law than many a college student.

At the end of a year, Henry applied for a license to practice law. According to the custom, three of the best lawyers in Virginia tested him, then signed his certificate. He was a full-fledged lawyer now.

Immediately, Henry brought his license to show Mr. Wythe.

"Henry Clay, gentleman," read the old man at the end of the document. He turned his head and coughed a little to hide the tears in his eyes. "Do you intend to practice in Richmond?" he asked.

"No, sir," said Henry. "I couldn't compete with fine lawyers like yourself."

"Tut! Tut!" said the old man. "You have youth and vision on your side. But where will you go?"

"To Lexington, Kentucky. My folks live near there. My stepfather owns an inn and is doing very well."

"You will have no trouble finding legal work in Kentucky," said Mr. Wythe. "There are hundreds of debates over land claims."

"My brother John wrote and told me that I could make five hundred dollars a year," said Henry.

"That should be ample to support you," said Mr. Wythe. "Nevertheless, I'll give you letters to my lawyer friends who have gone there. These letters will tell them about you. They will help you find a job in the beginning."

CHAPTER 7

Young Henry
of the West

We're all doing well here," said Captain Watkins when Henry arrived in Kentucky. "This is the greatest state in the Union."

The Watkins family lived in Versailles, which was about fourteen miles from Lexington. The Captain owned an inn and about a thousand acres of land and was a justice of the peace. John and Porter Clay were already established in Lexington.

"You can be a great lawyer in Kentucky now," said Henry's mother. "I always knew it would happen."

"I'll have to learn about court customs here before I begin to practice," said Henry. "But I'll hang out my shingle soon."

After a few days' visit with his family, Henry rode into Lexington. It was the most important town west of the Allegheny Mountains. Neat stores and houses lined its planked sidewalks. It had a three-story stone courthouse. On the hill were the brick buildings of Transylvania Seminary, the first college in the West.

Henry found lodgings and soon called on the lawyers to whom he had letters from Mr. Wythe.

"I'll be glad to have you work for me," said John Breckinridge. "I would have to be four people to handle all my cases."

Henry's first job was to collect a bill from a blacksmith who lived on the edge of town.

"It won't be easy," said Mr. Breckinridge. "I've done everything except send out the Kentucky militia after him."

There was a group of men around the smithy's place when Henry rode into the village. They were grumbling because they had come to hear an election speech and the speaker had not arrived.

"Can you speak a piece, stranger?" one man asked Henry.

"There's nothing I like better," he answered. In a few minutes, Henry was standing up in a wagon and making a rousing speech about Daniel Boone, whom all the mountaineers loved.

"Best speech I've heard in years," roared the blacksmith when Henry stopped. "What's your name, stranger?"

"Henry Clay, and I've come to collect the money you owe Lawyer Breckinridge."

In a few minutes, the blacksmith came out with a bag of cut silver. "Here's your money," he said. "I'm glad you spoke on our side."

So Henry rode back to Lexington not knowing on which side he had spoken. But his first fee as a lawyer would soon be in his pocket.

It was not long before Henry joined the debating club in Lexington. He had been urged to join by a young lawyer friend, John Brown.

At the first meeting Henry attended, the

members were debating a bill to free the slaves
in Kentucky. Henry had always felt deeply
on this subject. He had never forgotten his
attempt to help Dilsey escape.

The debate on slavery was about to be closed
when Henry raised his hand. The chairman
at once invited him to speak.

For a minute, Henry was uncertain. This
was his first speech to such a group.

"Gentlemen of the jury," he began.

Everyone laughed, but in good humor.

"You're not defending a client," said John
Brown with a grin.

But the good-natured teasing of the crowd
gave Henry confidence.

He spoke earnestly and well. The laughter
died down. Everyone leaned forward so as
not to miss a word, though the rich golden
voice of the speaker could be heard easily in
the farthest corner of the room.

His eyes blazed. The color was bright in
his cheeks. His tall, slim figure moved grace-
fully. His long, white hands made meaning-
ful gestures. There were roars of applause

from the audience when Henry sat down.

"We'll vote for freedom of the slaves at the next meeting of the legislature," everybody promised him.

"You have a great gift," said John Brown as they were going home. "A person with a voice and manner like yours can make men do anything."

It was not long before Henry was a favorite with everyone. Old people liked him because he was thoughtful and kind and interested in their affairs. He was a leader among the young men. They liked his friendliness, his gaiety, his quick wit, and hearty laughter. He was generous and helpful to all. Even the people who lived on the frontier liked Henry. He met them when he rode out on circuit to defend them in court. They thought he was a fine young gentleman, but he always listened to what they had to say. He slept in their homes and ate their rough food, and never failed to show how grateful he was for their hospitality.

With the girls in Lexington, Henry was as

popular as he had been in Richmond. The clothes he wore with such a fine air won him their admiring looks. His graceful dancing, the compliments he paid them, and his charming manners won their hearts. Nor did the mothers of Lexington discourage Henry because he lacked money. He was earning good fees already, and in the West every man had a chance to win a fortune.

But there was one girl whom Henry singled out from the beginning. She was Lucretia Hart, the daughter of Colonel Thomas Hart, a wealthy merchant and banker in Lexington. Henry's best friend, James Brown, was married to Lucretia's sister Nancy. Lucretia was slim and graceful, with red-brown hair, dark eyes, and delicate features. She and Henry fell in love almost as soon as they met. They were married in Lucretia's home on April 11, 1799.

This was the beginning of success in other ways for Henry. He received his license to practice law in Kentucky and opened an office. Soon he was as busy as Lawyer Breckinridge.

Henry's first big case was to defend Dorshey Phelps, a woman who had shot and killed
her sister-in-law. Dorshey confessed the crime
as soon as she was caught. Her husband had
asked Henry to take her case.

"But she confessed," said Henry. "She's
certain to be hanged."

"That's what I'm afraid of," said her husband. "And it's not right. My sister was always
nagging Dorshey about the way she spent our
money. Dorshey helped to earn that money.
And she's always had a mighty hot temper."

"But that's no excuse for killing," said
Henry. "I'll have to find a better reason."

Henry talked the case over with Lucretia.

"There's nothing makes a woman more
furious than to have her in-laws nag her about
money," said Lucretia. "I'd lose my mind,
too."

Henry looked thoughtfully at his wife.
"You have given me an idea," he said.

The future looked very dark for Dorshey
Phelps three days later in the crowded courtroom in Lexington. Henry made no attempt

to defend her crime. His only witness was Mr. Phelps. Most of Henry's questions dealt with the way the sister-in-law nagged Dorshey about spending money.

At the end of the trial, Henry walked over to the jury box to make his closing speech. "Gentlemen," he said gravely. "This is a shocking case."

The jurymen looked at each other in surprise. Was the defense giving up so quickly?

"A woman who was always known to be a good mother and a devoted wife has committed a terrible crime," Henry continued. "Look at her now, gentlemen," he said sadly.

The jurors strained forward. Those standing in the courtroom stretched on tiptoe. Dorshey sat huddled in her chair. Big tears were slowly rolling down her cheeks.

"Look at her now, gentlemen," Henry repeated. "Her eyes are wild. She is frightened at her thoughts. She cannot believe that she was the one who did that terrible deed." Henry's eyes blazed as he spoke. There were high spots of color in his cheeks. His slender,

white hand pointed at Dorshey and then at his hearers.

"It was not Dorshey Phelps," Henry continued in a thundering voice. "It was not the woman we know who committed that crime. It was another Dorshey Phelps who, in a moment of temporary insanity — temporary insanity," slowly Henry repeated the phrase, "did what she now considers as awful a deed as do all you understanding and sympathetic neighbors."

The jurors looked at each other and then stared at the victim of this new kind of mental trouble. In a low voice, Henry continued his plea for the life of his client. "If Dorshey's husband has forgiven her," he concluded, "surely her twelve good neighbors can be equally merciful."

Manslaughter was the verdict of the jurors, and five years in prison the sentence for Dorshey Phelps.

Henry's career as a criminal lawyer had begun. From that day on, he rarely lost a case. And a new reason for the crime of taking a life was started in the history of the law courts.

There were other stories about trials in which Henry Clay took part that became legal legends in Kentucky.

Once he questioned a witness in the case of Jim Barton, a mountaineer who was being sued for money he owed to some merchants in Lexington.

"Jim Barton is slow to pay what he owes," said the witness angrily.

Henry came over to the witness box and leaned forward, so that he could look directly at the man.

"Slow but sure," said Henry.

The witness moved uneasily. It was hard to look into those blue eyes of Henry Clay and not tell the truth.

"Slow but sure," repeated the witness.

One of the jurors, a storekeeper, gave a loud grunt.

Henry looked at him. The man had been chewing tobacco, and his white beard and mouth were stained with the brown juice.

Jim Barton has traded with him in the

past, thought Henry, *and Jim hasn't paid him on time.*

"Your witness," said Henry to the prosecutor.

But before sitting down, Henry stopped at the jury box. He made up his mind that he would win over the storekeeper to his side.

He bowed politely to the storekeeper. "I have forgotten my snuff box, Mr. Cooper," he said. "Could you let me have a pinch of snuff?"

Mr. Cooper felt in all his pockets. Everybody was on tiptoe in the courthouse to see what was happening. The prosecutor waited impatiently.

Finally, Mr. Cooper pulled a wad of dark tobacco from his pocket and offered it to Henry.

"I don't snuffs, but I chaws, Mr. Clay," he said.

Henry broke off a piece of tobacco and bowed his thanks.

The old storekeeper sat up straight and wiped the dribbles of tobacco juice from his mouth. He looked toward the table. That fine young Mr. Clay was chewing some of Joe Cooper's home-cured tobacco. Maybe Mr. Clay was right to say Jim Barton was "slow but sure" to pay his debts.

When the Clays were first married, they lived in a small brick house next to Colonel Hart's. But Henry was eager to buy land on the outskirts of Lexington.

"I want to have a fine plantation and a home like the great planters in Virginia," he told his young wife.

In 1803, Henry was elected to the legislature of Kentucky which met in Frankfort, the capital. He became a leader in most of the debates. There was never a day now when he did not make a speech. In 1806, he was chosen Speaker of the House in Kentucky, a very important job.

Henry was making money, too. In 1806, his dream of owning a big plantation came true. He bought a farm of two hundred and fifty acres about a mile and a half from Lexington.

"What shall we call our place, dear?" Henry asked Lucretia, the first time they drove out to inspect their farm.

She looked at the thick grove of ash trees on the rise of ground on which they were standing.

"Why not call it 'Ashland'?" she suggested.

Henry thought that was a wonderful name.

"We'll build a fine house on this rise of

land," he planned. "And I'll breed pedigreed horses and cattle. I'll have my own race track at the foot of this hill so that I can train the horses."

"There is no better food for cattle than the bluegrass of Kentucky," said Lucretia.

Henry nodded. The grass had a bluish color so that Kentucky people called their land "bluegrass country."

Henry and his friends had started a Jockey Club in Lexington. They had regular racing meets now, just as in Richmond.

"The only way to encourage the breeding of fine horses is to have racing meets," said Henry. "Some day the finest horses in the country will come from Kentucky."

CHAPTER 8

"So This Is Washington!"

In 1806, Henry Clay was elected to fill out the term of General Adair, who had resigned from the United States Senate. At that time, a United States senator was elected by the legislature of his state.

About a month later Henry left for Washington, as Congress was in session. He traveled by stagecoach and horseback, and it took him several weeks to make the journey.

On the morning of December twenty-ninth, Henry stopped his horse near the top of Capitol Hill in Washington, so that he could look over the city. "So this is Washington!" he exclaimed half aloud.

The city had been planned by L'Enfant, a

famous engineer. But Henry shook his head at the dismal sight before him. The trees and bushes were bare from the cold weather, but so was the hill on which he stood, and the rest of the area as far as he could see. At the top of the hill, masons were working on the half-finished Capitol building. Near it were some shabby wooden buildings. Most of these were small inns and boarding houses.

Yesterday, Henry had ridden from Georgetown along a wide, muddy road. It was called Pennsylvania Avenue, and he had passed the President's Mansion where Thomas Jefferson now lived. But there were only a few other buildings along the avenue. Most of the lawmakers lived in the boarding houses near the Capitol.

"Well, it may be a great city some day," said Henry to himself. "But it doesn't compare with Lexington."

In the Senate Chamber, Henry was given a desk in the back of the room on the Republican side. He was a member of the Republican party. (This is not the Republican party of today, but the party started by Jefferson. Later the party members called themselves Democrats.) After the opening proceedings were over, Henry was escorted to the platform where the Vice President, who presided over the Senate, was seated.

"I wish to present Henry Clay, the new senator from Kentucky," said the senior senator from Henry's home state.

Then a senator from the Federalist side, which was the opposing party, rose to protest.

"There is a report that the junior senator from Kentucky is not yet thirty years old, which is the age required by the Constitution," said he.

"What have you to say to that, Mr. Clay?" asked the Vice President.

Everyone turned to look at Henry as he rose. He was tall and slim, and fine-looking in his new blue broadcloth coat. He seemed even younger than he was. He wouldn't be thirty until April. But the legislature in Kentucky had not questioned his age, and he had not given it a thought.

111

"I suggest that the senator ask the people of Kentucky," said Henry politely. "They sent me here."

His fine rich voice reached to every part of the room. The members of his party brightened as they looked at him. Some were grinning at his answer. Everyone in that room knew that by the time a messenger was sent to Kentucky and returned, Henry would have reached the required age.

Since there was no further protest, he was sworn into office.

On New Year's Day, Henry went to the President's Mansion for the reception. The day was warm and sunny. The sun glittered on the big sandstone house. The East Room was filled with gaily dressed people, and the red-coated Marine Band played on the lawn.

President Jefferson greeted Henry warmly. They recalled the times they had met when Henry had been secretary to Mr. Wythe. The President was interested in Henry's political success, especially since he belonged to Jefferson's own Republican party.

Then Henry moved to the dining room where the tables were laden with cakes, candies, mounds of ice cream, and silver bowls of punch. It was the first time he had eaten ice cream, and he enjoyed each cold, delicious mouthful.

This was the first of many pleasant times Henry had in Washington. He met many well-known people — Robert Fulton, the young artist and inventor; Benjamin Latrobe, the architect who had designed part of the Capitol; and Washington Irving, a lively young reporter from New York.

But Henry was glad when the session of Congress came to a close on March fourth. He was much more interested in the politics of his own state than in national affairs.

He was concerned, too, about his wife, Lucretia. They were expecting their fifth child in April. Their first little girl had died. The other three children — Theodore, Thomas, and Susan — had been lively and well when Henry had left home. Were they still in good health? Letters traveled so slowly that the last

114

news he had had was several weeks old.

"Kentucky is still my favorite state," Henry wrote in a letter to Colonel Hart telling of his homecoming. "I am glad to be going home."

In 1810, Henry served again in the United States Senate. This time he was deeply interested in what was going on in Washington. The whole country was angered because Great Britain interfered with our merchant ships. The people of the West were especially angry at the British. They felt the British in Canada were to blame for the Indian attacks on the frontier states.

"I am for resistance by the sword," cried Henry in a speech in the Senate.

There were amazed looks from the older senators who believed in caution.

Henry was aware of this feeling.

"The Senate is too slow moving for me," he said to a friend. "I would rather be a member of the House. I shall announce myself as a candidate this summer."

In the election of August, 1810, Henry Clay was the only candidate from his district in Kentucky. All others had withdrawn when he had stated his intention to run. With no opposition, he was elected to the Twelfth Congress of the United States.

There were seventy new representatives, out of one hundred and forty-two, in the House of Representatives in 1811. Most of these were young men from the West and South. Many had never been in Washington before. One new member was Henry Clay from Kentucky. Another was John C. Calhoun from South Carolina. He was only twenty-nine. A man could become a member of the House after he had reached the age of twenty-five. Calhoun was tall and thin with a great mass of brown hair swept back from his forehead, and he had dark, deep-set eyes. He and Henry were to be part of our national government for more than forty years.

The business of swearing in the new members was quickly finished on the first day of the session. At once, the Chairman announced that the Speaker of the House would now be elected.

"I nominate Henry Clay of Kentucky," shouted a member.

"I second the nomination," cried Calhoun.

There was loud applause.

Henry stood up and bowed. His wide mouth was spread in a grin of delight.

The voting started. Henry was far in the lead by the time half the names had been called. By the end of the roll call, he had a two-to-one lead over his nearest opponent.

"It is the first time in our history that a Speaker was elected in his first term in office!" Henry's supporters exclaimed joyfully.

Henry strode to the platform and took the oath of office. Then he stood in front of the Speaker's chair to address the House. Above him was a red and green velvet canopy fringed in gold, and over this was a large stone eagle with outspread wings.

The sunshine streamed into the room through the skylight in the roof. It brightened the Speaker's tall slim figure and blond hair. He smiled at the large group to his right who were members of his own party.

Then he heard a high, angry voice from the Federalist side of the House. "The war hawks are flying over us. Mark my words, we shall have war before this session is over."

The color rose in Henry's cheeks. "War hawks!" So that was what his opponents were calling the men like himself who thought that the United States should declare war on Great Britain. He was thinking of the time when he was a small boy and Tarleton had insulted the grave of John Clay. *Did my bitterness against the British start then?*

But he smiled pleasantly at his audience. "I wish to thank the members present for the honor they have given me," said the Speaker.

Bills! Bills! Bills! They were passed quickly in the House and sent to the Senate. All of them had to do with making the country ready for war. All were made into law.

For a time, President Madison, who hoped for a peaceful settlement, held out against the pressure. At last, however, he sent a message to Congress giving his reasons for war. By the middle of June, 1812, the United States had declared war against Great Britain.

The war went badly for the United States, though our privateers did much damage to the British merchant fleet. In the spring of 1813, Henry Clay was sent to Europe to help make a peace treaty. In Ghent, Belgium, he met our other agents, among whom were John Quincy Adams and Albert Gallatin.

The peace meetings dragged on for months. Adams was almost willing to accept the British terms, although they meant loss for us. But Henry Clay urged him to wait.

"I have been playing cards with the British agents," said Henry. "I have watched their faces when they are playing and when they are meeting with us. I think they are trying to bluff us. Let us wait a little longer."

Henry was right. The British were really anxious to have the war come to an end. Napoleon had escaped from the island of Elba and soon would renew his war against England. At last, the British agreed to our terms, and the peace treaty was signed on December 24, 1814.

Henry decided, as he sailed for home, that this had been a war of folly. How much better it would have been to try to settle the quarrels in a peaceful way! What had been gained except the knowledge that war was useless?

Well, we were a new nation, and we had defended our honor. We had shown that we could not be bullied by an older nation. Now we were no longer an infant nation. We could turn our backs on Europe and begin to spread to the West.

My West! My country! thought Henry Clay.

CHAPTER 9

The Missouri Compromise

The tall candles on Speaker Clay's desk in the House of Representatives burned low on the last day of 1819. It was almost midnight, and the members had been debating since noon. The two territories, Maine and Missouri, had asked to be admitted as states. But to the bill which would allow Missouri to become a state, Representative Talmadge had added a statement saying that if Missouri came in, no more slaveholders could settle there. This, in time, would end slavery in Missouri. The people of the South were very unhappy.

"Why should there be a condition for letting Missouri come in as a state, if Maine comes in with no condition?" asked the Southerners.

Even Henry Clay had taken part in the debate this day. He owned slaves, but he had always been against slavery. He hoped that some day slavery would end all over the country.

"Justice is due to all parts of the Union," said Henry at the end of a two-hour speech.

But Talmadge would not give in, and many Northerners in the House agreed with him. He insisted on making the last speech of the day.

"You have started a fire which only oceans of blood can put out," shouted one member to Talmadge.

"If civil war must come because of this," cried Talmadge, "I can only say, let it come."

Civil war! Those were wild words, thought Henry as the debate ended. Were a few hot-headed leaders in Congress to throw to the winds all that our forefathers had gained for us? Never, if he could prevent it. Dear as the South and West were to Henry Clay, there was something even more precious. And that was the Union: North, South, East and West — all one, all a great and glorious whole.

A week later, the Clays attended a state dinner at the White House. At the end of the meal, after the ladies had left the room, Henry moved his place. He wanted to speak to Senator Pinckney, who was the leader of the Southerners in the Senate. They were soon talking about the bills for the admission of Maine and Missouri.

"The Senate will never accept the bill," said Pinckney. "The South controls the vote. Missouri must come in as a slave state with no conditions."

"Wouldn't it be better to make a compromise?" asked Henry. "I suggest that we let Missouri come in as a slave state but agree not to let slavery spread to any more states."

Senator Pinckney could hardly believe his ears. "But I thought you were on the Southern side of the question," he said.

"I am. But not if it means civil war."

Senator Thomas from Illinois now leaned forward. "I have a compromise in mind, Mr. Clay," he said, "that I would like to talk over with you."

"Will you come to my office tomorrow, Senator Thomas?" asked Henry. "I will back anything that will save the Union."

By March 3, 1820, the Missouri Compromise had been passed. Missouri came in as a slave state and Maine as a free state. But in the rest of the Louisiana Purchase Territory there was to be a line at 36 degrees, 30 minutes. North of this line, except for Missouri, slavery was forbidden.

No more slave states will be formed from this day on, thought Henry, and he was happy to think that in time slavery might come to an end. *And there will be no civil war.*

At the end of that session of Congress, Henry resigned for a time. He was heavily in debt and needed to make money. "I shall have to work hard at my law practice," he told his wife.

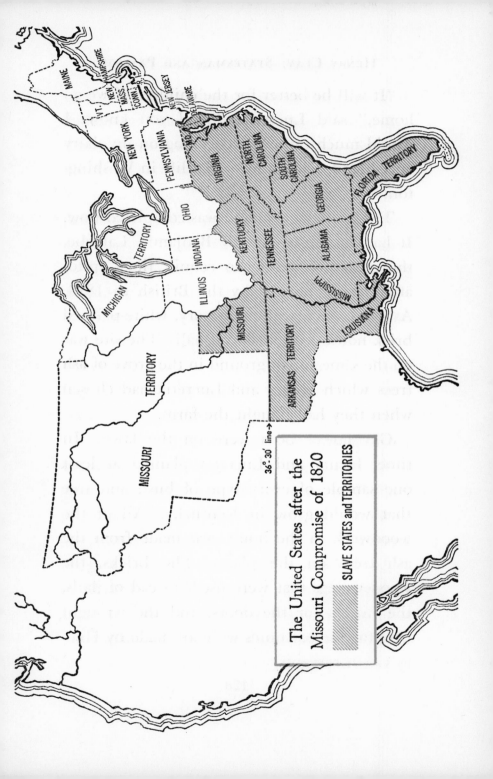

The United States after the
Missouri Compromise of 1820

SLAVE STATES and TERRITORIES

"It will be better for the children if we go home," said Lucretia. "And you know, I would much rather be checking on my dairy at Ashland than on my social life in Washington."

The house at Ashland was completed now. It had been planned by Benjamin Latrobe, the great architect who rebuilt the Capitol after it was burned by the British in 1814. Ashland was a wide, two-story, white-painted brick house with a central hall. The site was on the same rise of ground in the grove of ash trees which Henry and Lucretia had chosen when they had bought the farm.

Gay flower beds were on the lawn. In time, Henry and Lucretia planted at least one sample of every type of bush and tree that would grow in Kentucky. All of the woodwork in the house was made from the ash trees on the place. The bricks, the wooden pegs that were used instead of nails, the hinges for the doors, and the wrought iron for the balconies were all made by Henry's own servants.

It was not difficult for Henry to be happy at Ashland. As he had planned, he was raising purebred stock. In 1817 he had imported three Hereford cattle from England. They were the first to be raised in the United States. He had them brought by boat to Baltimore and then on foot across the Alleghenies. Next he had Merino sheep brought from Pennsylvania, as well as some purebred hogs.

There was nothing Henry enjoyed more than taking a long ear of corn and feeding it to his prize swine. "It reminds me of my boyhood days when I used to practice speechmaking on the pigs," he told his friends.

The mile-round race track at Ashland was finished. Each day at dawn, Henry sat on the fence rail while he checked Woodpecker, his first racing horse.

"Some day, this blue grass country will have the finest race horse farms in America," he told the horse lovers who visited Ashland.

But it was Lucretia who made the farm pay with the butter and milk she sold to the hotels in Lexington.

129

"Mr. Wilson says my milk and butter are the best he ever bought for the Phoenix Hotel," she told Henry proudly.

The Clay children loved Ashland. There were nine of them now. Two girls had died when they were babies. Theodore, who was nineteen, was the oldest, followed by Thomas, who was a year younger. Then came Susan, Anne, Lucretia, Henry Junior, Eliza, James, and the new baby, John. There was two years difference in age between them.

Susan, the oldest girl, was quite a young lady. She enjoyed the company of her brother's classmates at Transylvania College, and they liked her.

"I think Jefferson Davis is one of the nicest boys at Transylvania," Susan told her parents. "It's too bad he is so much younger than I am, because I think he is very handsome. He never has time for anything but books, though."

"He probably has more important things on his mind than girls," teased her father.

"If Jefferson is too young for Susan, you

130

could invite him for me when you have parties," Anne urged her mother.

"You'll have to wait another year for a beau," said her mother. "I have all I can do to watch out for Susan." Lucretia smiled at her daughters. "But I'll tell Theodore to invite Jefferson for supper on Sunday."

"You had better tell Thomas to invite Jefferson," said Henry to Lucretia after the girls had left. "I don't believe Theodore will be able to continue at school."

Lucretia's face grew white. "Do you mean Theodore won't grow out of his trouble?" she asked. Their oldest son had had a head injury in a fall when he was a child. Ever since, he had suffered from bad headaches followed by ugly spells of temper.

Henry shook his head. "I have talked to several doctors. They all have the same opinion. It won't be long, they tell me, before his bad temper may turn into something more violent." He put his arm around his wife. "It is a cross we'll have to bear, my dear."

With her head buried on Henry's shoulder,

131

Lucretia did not see the tears in her husband's eyes. He would wait until later, he had decided, to tell her that he had already made plans to have Theodore placed in the Lexington Asylum for the Insane.

The following spring, Martin Duralde of New Orleans came to visit at Ashland. From the moment of his arrival, Susan forgot all about the boys at Transylvania. On April twenty-second, the Clays saw the first of their daughters married.

"Now I'm the one who will have all the parties," said Anne. "But I won't be in such a hurry to get married." She kissed her father. "You're my best beau."

Henry gave Anne a hug. She was his favorite daughter. Of all his children, Anne seemed the most interested in all that he did. Every morning, when they were together, they went for a long horseback ride.

"Wait until another handsome young man comes from the South," said her mother. "That's what I used to say before your father came to Lexington."

The handsome young man did come, though a year and a half later. He was James Erwin from Tennessee, and he visited the Clays in October, 1823. After a courtship of only three weeks, James, who had urgent business at home, got permission to marry Anne and take her to Tennessee.

"I'll come back to you, Father," sobbed Anne when she was leaving. "James has promised to buy the plantation next to Ashland as soon as his estate is settled."

Perhaps it was because his family seemed to be slipping away from him that Henry had agreed to run as a representative earlier that year. Once again he was chosen Speaker by the vote of every member in the House.

"I thank you again for the great honor you have bestowed on me," he said in his opening speech in the House. "I trust that you will give me equal support in the election next November."

There was a new part in politics that Henry Clay had in mind for "next November."

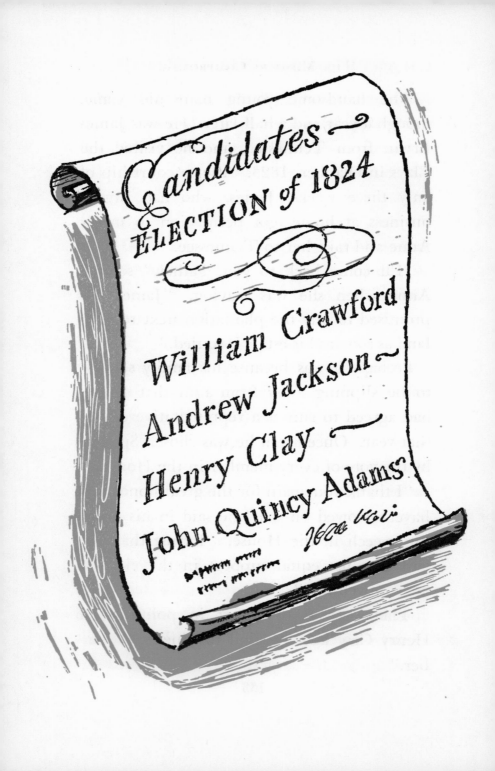

CHAPTER 10

King Maker

The new office which Henry sought in 1824 was the Presidency of the United States. It was an unusual election. The four men who were running were all from the same party. The only difference was that they were from different parts of the country. Henry Clay was from Kentucky, and Andrew Jackson was from Tennessee. William Crawford was from Georgia. John Quincy Adams was from Massachusetts; his father, John Adams, had been our second President.

To be elected President, one man had to get more votes than all the others put together. Because the vote was split among the four men who were running, no one man had enough votes to become President. Andrew Jackson had the largest number of votes.

In such a case, a President had to be elected by the House of Representatives. The President would be chosen from the three men who had the highest number of votes in the election. Here Henry was unlucky. He had lost the third place by four votes.

If I had won either in New York or Louisiana, I would be the next President, he thought bitterly as he traveled toward Washington late in December. He knew very well that the members of the House would have voted for their popular Speaker.

Then his heart lifted. "There will be other chances," he told himself. "This is only my first try."

From the day Henry arrived in Washington, the supporters of each of the three candidates tried to get his help.

"They must all believe I control the votes of my friends in the House," said Henry one day to a close friend. "They act as if I were a king maker."

"But don't you intend to vote for Adams?" asked his friend.

"I suppose so," said Henry. "Though I have never liked him."

"He might make you his Secretary of State if you support him," said the friend.

"I don't know whether I would like a Cabinet place," answered Henry. "I will vote for him because I believe in the things for which he stands. Crawford is a sick man, and Jackson is only a war hero. I can't see why killing 2500 men at the Battle of New Orleans makes a man fit for the Presidency."

No one guessed Henry Clay's own disappointment. He joked about his defeat and worked hard to win votes for Adams. But he wished that his family had come with him to Washington. Only to Lucretia could he tell his real feelings.

A heavy snow fell in Washington on the morning of February twelfth, the day on which the House was to vote for the President. The result, so far, was very close. It depended on the vote of New York. Here the vote was divided equally, and only one man, General Van Rensselaer, was still uncertain as to how he would vote in the election.

As the tall, white-haired old man walked into the House Chamber that morning, Henry hurried to greet him.

"You are covered with snow, General," he said. "Let me brush you off." Then as he helped the old man take off his coat, Henry added, "I hope you have considered my remarks in favor of Mr. Adams."

"I shall let God direct my choice," answered the General.

"I am sure then that you will vote for Mr.

Adams," said Henry. "Like yourself, he is a God-fearing man."

Finally, the balloting began. The small states soon finished, and their chairmen brought the ballots to a table in front of the room. Soon all were counted except New York.

The ballot box was passed from hand to hand. Finally, it reached Van Rensselaer. Everyone in the room became quiet and watched to see what he would do. All realized how important would be his choice. Henry's

hand tightened on the edge of his desk, as he in turn waited for the old man to act.

For a long half minute, General Van Rensselaer did nothing. Then he bowed his head in his hands, as if he were praying. Slowly he raised his head, and as he did so, his eyes grew wide. He was staring at a slip of paper on the floor in front of him.

From his desk, Henry could see that the paper was a half-torn ballot. But scrawled across it he read the name of Adams.

The old man nodded and smiled a little. His lips moved as if he prayed. But his face was calm. Quickly, he wrote something on his own ballot and dropped it into the box.

Ten minutes later, the result was read aloud. John Quincy Adams had the vote of 13 states; Jackson, 7; and Crawford, 4. Two days later, Adams announced that Henry Clay would be his Secretary of State.

The followers of Jackson were quick to cry that there had been a "bargain" between Clay and Adams. They kept this up for the next four years. The smartest newspapermen in the country backed Jackson. They never missed a chance to print stories showing that Henry Clay and the President were not honest in politics.

Henry was not happy as Secretary of State, although he did a fine job. He did not like the work, for he missed the excitement of open debate in Congress. But there was one reason why he did not resign. The place might lead to the Presidency.

"Jefferson, Madison, Monroe, and John Quincy Adams were all Secretaries of State," he told Lucretia. "It might be a stepping stone for me."

"There is no one in the party who is more popular or better fitted to be President than you," said his wife proudly.

Henry smiled. Lucretia's faith in him always warmed his heart. "But we need to win friends for the party," he said.

By this time, the followers of Andrew Jackson were calling themselves "Democrats," so the supporters of Adams called themselves "National Republicans."

"We ought to entertain a great deal," said Lucretia. "Especially since Mrs. Adams gives so few parties."

"You are right," Henry agreed. "More votes are won around the dinner table than any other place."

So the Clays rented a large three-story brick house on F street which was near the President's Mansion. There was scarcely a meal to which guests were not invited. Lucretia made many calls each day. The house on F Street was filled every night. The streets in the neighborhood were bright with the torches along the road and the lamps of the carriages that clattered to the door. Lucretia shuddered at the bills but did her best. This was part of her husband's political life. But she was happy when summer came, and they all returned to Ashland.

During his years as Secretary, Henry had much family unhappiness. The Clays' first sorrow had come in 1825. On their way to Washington, they had stopped at Lebanon, Ohio, because ten-year-old Eliza was ill with

fever. Although she grew steadily worse, Henry felt he must leave. He was never to see Eliza again. She died a few days later and was buried in Lebanon.

Nine months later, in September, 1825, came the second family tragedy. Their oldest daughter Susan, married to Martin Duralde of New Orleans, died there of yellow fever.

Nor did either Henry or Lucretia have much comfort in their older sons. Theodore, although well, was still in the asylum for the insane. But it was Thomas who caused his parents the most concern. He was always in debt, and once was arrested in Philadelphia for reckless conduct. Henry's chief pride was in his third and favorite son, Henry Junior. He had won an appointment to West Point and had a fine record.

"If you, too, disappoint my hopes," his father wrote to him, "I will sink beneath the pressure. The hopes of all of us are turned upon you."

The attacks of the followers of Jackson against Clay and President Adams increased as the election of 1828 drew near. In October, Henry still hoped that Adams would be re-elected, but Lucretia quietly prepared to leave Washington. About the middle of November, the results were known. Jackson had 178 votes and Adams, 83. The new Democratic party was in the saddle, and its President-General rode his horse high.

New sorrows were to greet the Clay family when they returned to Ashland. Within two weeks Henry's mother, his stepfather Captain Watkins, and his brother John all died. It was almost a relief for Henry that Ashland, which had been rented, needed so much work.

CHAPTER 11

The Great
Compromiser

Daniel Webster wrote a letter in 1831 to Henry, urging him to run again for the Senate.

"The election of 1832 is near," wrote Webster. "You are the one choice of our party. You should be in Washington to meet the enemy face to face."

The "enemy" was Andrew Jackson.

So Henry once again was elected to the Senate by the legislature of Kentucky, whose members were happy to see him willing to serve the state. He planned to work for laws which he thought would keep the country united, and to use his position to fight President Jackson.

147

Henry had never forgotten how difficult it had been to trade when he was a clerk at Denny's store in Richmond. There were three laws which he thought would make trading easier. First, he wanted a bank controlled by the United States Government, so that the paper money used would have the same value all over the country. Second, he wanted a high tariff (which would mean a high tax set on goods sent here from foreign countries), so that foreign goods would not be cheaper than goods made in the United States. Finally, he thought that if good, wide roads were built by the national government, products could be carried more easily.

The Congressmen from the South fought against the tariff.

"You will ruin the South if you get your way," a man from South Carolina told Clay. "The South has to buy all of its manufactured goods, but it sells only raw products."

"The whole country will be helped if we have a high tariff — plus good roads," answered Henry. "Then you can sell your raw

stuff to the North and buy back the manufactured things you need. That will make us
a united country. We will depend on no one."

"But we'll pay more for what we buy," said
the Southerner. "It's about time that the
South began to think whether it is important
to remain in the United States. We can set
up our own government, you know."

"Don't talk so wildly," said Henry. He
hoped that what he had heard was only the
opinion of a few hot-headed people.

Henry Clay worked hard, and all three bills
were passed by Congress. But Jackson did
not sign the bills for the bank and the building of roads. Only the Tariff Bill of 1832 became a law.

"Wait until the election in November,"
said the friends of Henry Clay. "New York
and Pennsylvania want the bank. And Jackson can't be elected without their votes."

But the people of New York and Pennsylvania wanted their war-hero President more
than they wanted the bank. When the votes
were counted, there were 219 for Jackson and

49 for Clay. It was Henry Clay's worst defeat.

After the election Henry tried to resign from the Senate. "Of what use am I either to Kentucky or the nation?" he asked his friends.

However, he gave in to their pleas and promised to remain in Congress for a time. He made this promise because he was concerned about something that had happened.

Late in November, South Carolina announced that the state would not obey the Tariff Law of 1832. If forced to do so, South Carolina would leave the Union. To be ready for this, the Governor of South Carolina called for a volunteer army.

Almost at once, President Jackson sent out a Proclamation: "Disunion by armed force is treason," it stated. The President asked Congress to give him the authority to send troops into South Carolina to collect the tariffs.

In the Senate Chamber on the opening day of Congress, Henry discussed what had happened with a friend, John Clayton.

"I think the people of South Carolina are worried," said Henry. "Look at Calhoun's face."

"They probably thought they could bluff Congress into doing away with the tariff law," said Clayton. "They didn't count on what Jackson would do."

"Jackson is probably worried, too," said Henry. "Sending troops into South Carolina might start a war between the states."

"Can't you think of a way out of this?" asked Clayton. "You got us out of the trouble over Missouri in 1820."

"I could ask to have the tariff lowered. Maybe that would satisfy South Carolina."

"Well, why not do that?" asked Clayton hopefully.

Henry Clay shook his head. "If I do that, all the people who believe as I do in a high tariff will turn against me. I've been for a high tariff first, last, and always."

"But if you don't, this nation might be destroyed," said John Clayton earnestly. "You are the only one in Congress who is

151

powerful enough to make both sides agree."

"I'll see Calhoun tomorrow," said Henry with a sigh. "Then I'll see Webster. He stands for a high tariff."

Both Calhoun and Webster finally agreed to compromise. Webster wanted the Union to last. Calhoun feared civil war for his state.

The Compromise Tariff Bill of 1833 was passed. Each side had given up certain things to get the compromise bill accepted. The rates would be lowered each year until they were the same as the low rates of 1816.

Tired, but happy that he had succeeded, Henry went home to Ashland. Everywhere he was greeted as the "Great Compromiser."

"South Carolina was not bluffing," the people told him. "We would have had a war between the states."

To himself Henry said, "I won't get the high tariff in which I believe, but I have saved the Union." Perhaps he would lose followers, too, and even the Presidency. It was at this time that he wrote a letter to a friend, saying at the end of it, "I would rather be right than President."

He remembered how he had wanted to resign after Jackson had defeated him. He decided that as long as the people of Kentucky wanted him to do so, he would remain in the Senate. There he would work for the laws which he thought were best for the country.

The people who supported Henry Clay grew more and more bitter against Andrew Jackson during his second term.

"He acts as if he were a king," they said. "He is even planning to have Martin Van Buren succeed him as if the Presidency were inherited."

The newspapers opposed to Jackson began printing cartoons showing Jackson dressed as a king, with a crown and ermine-trimmed robes, and carrying a sceptre. "King Andrew, the Tyrant," was the title.

"We are like the Whigs in England who fought against the tyranny of King George the Third," said Henry. "We should call ourselves the Whig party."

"And the Democrats are the Tories," said a listener.

In letters and speeches from then on, Henry Clay called his followers "Whigs." Gradually, everyone used the name.

But Henry was to put politics aside for a little while because of a great personal loss. In December, 1835, he was attending a Christmas party in Washington and was in the best of spirits when a letter was brought to him.

"It is too bad Lucretia isn't here," he said as he broke the seal. "We have been waiting for this letter. It's from James Erwin, the husband of my daughter Anne. She's going to have a baby."

Then he quickly read the single page. His face grew white as he let the sheet of paper drop from his hand. A moment later, he fell back into a chair.

John Clayton, who was nearby, picked up the letter. "Anne died when the child was born," said he. "Now God give Henry Clay courage."

It was days before Henry saw anyone but his close friends. To them, he talked only of his deep sorrow. Lucretia remained in her room, praying or reading from the Bible.

"Now they are all gone — all my lovely daughters," said Henry to John Clayton. "And to lose Anne! Why, John, it is as if I had lost a piece of my soul. She was so good, so dutiful, so loving. She has been so much a part of every plan I have made for the remainder of my years, that I feel now there is nothing left for me."

Andrew Jackson was still powerful enough in 1836 to have Van Buren elected by a large majority. The day of Martin Van Buren's inauguration was bright with sunshine. Jackson rode with him in a carriage to the Capitol and looked as happy as the newly elected President himself.

As Henry came out of the Senate Chamber that day, he met Tom Ritchie, his boyhood friend of Richmond days. Tom was an editor now of a Richmond paper and had come to Washington for the inauguration.

"Time is dealing gently with you, Henry," said Tom.

Henry threw out both his hands as if to push Father Time away. I'll keep the Old Fellow off as long as I can," he promised with a grin.

The meeting raised his spirits. For the first time since Anne's death, he felt cheerful. It was true that he was sixty years old. But he was still young in looks and spirit — hadn't Tom Ritchie said that? — young enough to look forward to the election of 1840. And why not?

CHAPTER 12

"I Would Rather Be Right..."

A young friend slowly made his way to Henry Clay's lodgings on a spring evening in 1840.

"Who was nominated?" Henry asked him quickly. He knew the young man had been waiting at the railroad station to hear the news from the men who were coming back from the Whig convention in Harrisburg, Pennsylvania.

The visitor did not answer at once. He hated to tell the news. "Harrison was named for the Presidency," he said at last. "John Tyler was nominated for Vice President."

Henry's face grew red with anger. He threw up his arms in disgust. "I am the most unlucky man in politics!" he cried. "I am nominated by my friends when I am sure to lose. And now they turn against me, when any Whig could win."

"But your friends didn't turn against you," said the young man. "Many of them wept when they voted for Harrison."

"Then why didn't they vote for me? What good are tears?"

"They nominated Harrison because he is a war hero."

Henry nodded. General William Henry Harrison was the hero of the Battle of Tippecanoe in the War of 1812. "They think the voters want another Andrew Jackson," he said bitterly.

"Will you work to have Harrison elected?" asked the young man anxiously. He liked Henry Clay very much, but he wanted the Whigs to win the election. "You have said publicly that you would sacrifice yourself for the good of the party."

The high color in Henry's face died down. He was remembering the letter he wrote in

1832. "I would rather be right than President," he had written. This time he had promised to support whoever was chosen by the party.

"I meant what I said," he answered slowly. "I'll work for Harrison."

Henry Clay was one of many who worked hard in the campaign and was successful in getting William Henry Harrison elected President. Harrison was the first Whig President and was elected by a big majority. The Whigs also gained control of Congress. Henry remained in the Senate.

"I have more power in Congress than in the Cabinet," he told his friends, who still thought he was the real leader of the party.

A cold wind blew on the inauguration day, and a light rain fell all morning. But Harrison rode on his fine white horse and refused to wear an overcoat or a hat. The Democrats had called him "Granny Harrison" all during the campaign, and he was determined to show that he had the strength for the office.

161

Three weeks later, President Harrison became ill with pneumonia, and he died on April fourth. He was the first President to die in office, and John Tyler was the first Vice President to succeed to the Presidency in this way.

Control of Congress by the Whigs for the next four years was of little help to their party. President Tyler refused to sign several bills that Congress approved.

"The biggest mistake we made was not to nominate you in 1840," said one of the leaders of the party to Henry Clay.

"We'll not make that same mistake in 1844," said another.

Henry bowed and smiled, for he knew what they meant.

1844! Another election year! The Whigs would certainly win. *And I shall be the candidate,* thought Henry.

A crowd was gathered at the station in Washington on the evening of May 1, 1844. Most of the men wore coon skin caps. A few carried big, wooden-framed, square boxes covered with thin cotton cloth. A light was inside the squares. Printed on the sides were the words, "We want Clay." Some of the cotton-covered boxes had a picture of a raccoon stretched on the limb of a tree, but with the face of Henry Clay. Someone started the new song,

The moon was shining silver bright.
The stars with glory crowned the night.
High on a limb that "same old coon,"
Was singing to himself this tune:
"Get out of the way, you're all unlucky.
Clear the way for old Kentucky."

"Clear the way for old Kentucky," yelled the crowd again and again. "We want Clay!"

They were waiting for the train to come in from Baltimore with the men who had been at the Whig convention.

Suddenly a boy rushed into the station waving a piece of paper. He was a messenger from the Capitol. "Clay was nominated on the first ballot!" he cried.

Roars of joy went up from the crowd. Then almost as quickly, the noise died down.

163

"How does that boy know? Did the train come in?" the men asked each other.

"He said he got it off the telegraph wire," said one man.

"Telegraph wire? What's that?"

"Sam Morse's invention. It's in the basement of the Capitol. He got it ready for the convention."

For a moment, even Henry Clay was forgotten with the strange news. It was wonderful! It was exciting! But it was frightening.

At the end of May the Democrats had their convention. This time the crowd waited outside the Capitol to hear the news over the telegraph. James K. Polk, a man who was almost unknown, was named instead of Van Buren.

"Who is Polk?" asked the Whigs. "What chance has he to win over Henry Clay, the best-loved man in the country?"

In high joy Henry returned to Ashland, for he refused to campaign for himself. The main question at the time was the annexation of Texas. James Polk was in favor of this, but

Henry Clay had always been opposed.

"If we annex Texas, we are bound to have a war with Mexico," he said, "and new slave states will be made."

"But the South will vote for Polk if you don't say Texas should be annexed," said his followers.

So Henry wrote a letter which was printed in the newspapers. "I am in favor of annexing Texas, if it can be done without dishonor and without war," it stated.

No one was quite sure of Henry Clay's views from what he wrote in this letter. People said that Clay wasn't taking a firm stand or that he was "sitting on the fence."

Results of the election came in slowly because the voting was done on different days in November. New York was the last important state to vote.

Henry heard the news from New York while he was attending a wedding party with Lucretia in Lexington. About ten o'clock in the evening, some of the men at the party went to the station to meet the train which

brought the newspapers from New York.
James K. Polk had won by 5,100 votes.

Henry read the headlines slowly when he
was handed a newspaper. As his friends
watched him, they saw his face turn almost
blue as if with cold. Finally, he smiled a little
and poured a glass of wine.

"I drink to the health of all assembled
here," he said clearly, as he lifted the glass.

Women in the room began to weep. The
men came up to Henry to shake his hand and

say something about their shock and grief. Somehow, he managed to return each warm handclasp.

At last, he and Lucretia left the party and drove to Ashland. In the quiet of their own hallway, Henry broke down and sobbed his disappointment.

"Promise me never again to try for the Presidency," begged Lucretia. "I cannot bear to see you hurt in this way."

"I need not promise. I am sixty-seven years old," said her husband.

Lucretia was the only one who saw Henry Clay's deep grief. He answered without bitterness the hundreds of letters and telegrams that came to him. They told of the sorrow all over the country. Men and women wept openly, and there were street fights when anyone spoke harshly of Henry Clay.

Henry's funds were low after the election of 1844. He had spent money on the campaign, and he had not earned much with his law practice. In addition, a note came due which Henry had signed to buy a plantation

home for Anne. At the same time, his son
Thomas was in debt for over $30,000. So
Henry borrowed money from a bank in Lex-
ington and put a mortgage on Ashland.

One day, when he tried to make a small
payment on the loan, the banker refused the
money.

"Why?" asked Henry. He thought there
could be nothing wrong, for the banker was
smiling.

"Because the loan is paid up."

"But how could that be? This is my first
payment."

"I have received gifts of money for you
from all over the country," said the banker.

Henry Clay tried his best to learn who had
given the money, but the banker said he was
sworn to secrecy. "One thing is sure, Mr.
Clay," he said, "the men who sent the
money were not your enemies."

At first Henry refused. During all his
political life, he had never taken a penny for
services or favors. But his friends urged him
to accept the money. "In all days, important

public service has been rewarded by gifts," they reasoned.

Next Henry consulted with Calvin Colton, a young professor who was writing a biography of him.

"I do not think you should feel embarrassed, Mr. Clay," said Colton. "Why should a man of your talents be in debt in his old age? If you had devoted your time to the law instead of service to your country, you would be a millionaire today."

So Henry Clay accepted the money in the fine spirit in which it had been offered. And he always felt deeply grateful for the gifts given by the unknown friends.

It was fortunate for Henry that he had this comfort, for he was soon to have another family loss. His son Henry Junior, who had resigned from the Army and had been practicing law for several years, went into the Army again when the Mexican War began in 1846. Like his father, Henry Junior wanted to be of service to his country. Stories of our brilliant victories in Mexico came to Lexington that winter. Then late in February of the following year came the news of the Battle of Buena Vista. The name of Lieutenant-Colonel Henry Clay Junior was at the top of the list of those who died in battle.

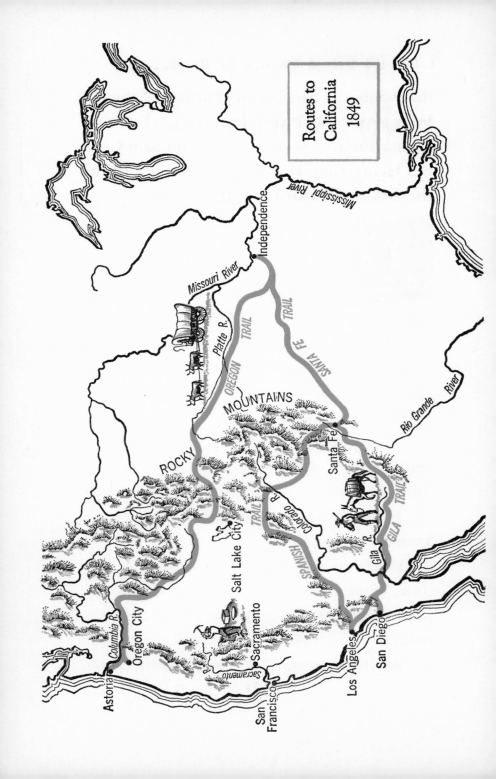

CHAPTER 13

"No North —
No South..."

In the early fall of 1849 the newspapers were filled with stories of the rush to California for gold. Soon came the news that the Californians had drawn up a constitution and wanted to come into the Union as a free state.

"That will end the balance in the Senate," said Henry to his son James, who was now his law partner in Lexington.

"Then the South will fight again," said James.

"I believe the South should give in this time," said Henry slowly. "None of the people who have gone out to California are slaveholders."

"We'll have a war between the states if the

South is forced to give in," said James.

"I'll do what I can in the Senate to prevent that," said his father.

The legislature of Kentucky once more had elected Henry Clay to the Senate, and he had agreed to serve another term.

On the opening day of the session of Congress, Henry saw many men who were well-known to him. Daniel Webster was there, and so was John C. Calhoun.

"We have been in Congress together for nearly forty years," said Henry as he greeted them.

Henry thought that Calhoun looked old and quite ill. His thick hair was still swept back from his high forehead, but it was iron-gray now. His skin was like old brown parchment and was stretched tight over his bony face.

Henry caught a glimpse of himself in a mirror and smiled, because he had thought that Calhoun looked old. "I'm nearly seventy-two," he remembered. He saw that he was growing bald and that his hair fell in thin, almost-white locks to his shoulders. His cheeks were hollow and his face had deep lines. But others who saw him also noticed that he stood tall and erect. The light still sparkled in his merry blue eyes, and his friendly smile had its old charm.

Wherever Henry moved in the Senate, men gathered around him and there was laughter, for he always had new stories to tell. "What are your plans for this session?" they asked him.

"I'll just pour oil on troubled waters," he said. "I'll certainly not make many speeches. I have a troublesome cough."

There were some new men Henry noticed in the Senate who were rapidly becoming important. There was William H. Seward of New York, who was the leader of those who wanted to end slavery. Another senator was big, tall Sam Houston of Texas, who led the war for his state's independence from Mexico. Jefferson Davis of Mississippi was the leader of the Southern slaveholders.

Most popular among the new men was

175

Stephen A. Douglas of Illinois. He was short and heavy, with a big head and thick, dark hair. Men called him "the little giant." His full rich voice could be heard all over the room.

He's like Daniel Webster, thought Henry. *Douglas will be the leader when we are gone.*

Henry thought that all the members in the Senate now seemed more solemn looking. Nowhere in the room did he see the bright colors of the high-collared, close-fitting coats that men had worn when first he had come to Washington. Instead, the senators wore long-skirted, black broadcloth coats and trousers of the same color.

Nor were there any ruffled shirts or muslin ties. Now the high stiff collars of the white shirts that the men wore were wound around with black silk scarves tied in a loose knot in the front. Almost every senator had a thick gold watch chain across his chest. Not a single one had a beard or mustache. Those were seen only on foreign diplomats.

But the room in which they were meeting

had not changed very much. The members still huddled near the blazing hickory fires. Those who were farther away pulled heavy woolen shawls over their shoulders and fastened them with big safety pins. Page boys moved briskly from desk to desk, filling the snuff boxes or putting fresh quill pens and ink in place. Only a few of the younger men used the new-fangled steel pens.

Slavery was the only topic discussed that session in Congress. Not only was there a bill to admit California as a state in which slavery would not be allowed, but there were also several other bills that had to do with slavery.

John C. Calhoun and Jefferson Davis took the side of the South in all the debates. William Seward was one of the leaders from the North. Neither side would give in on any measure. President Zachary Taylor favored the North. He was a slaveholder, but he was under the influence of Seward, who had helped to get Taylor elected.

"The North has nothing to lose," argued

Calhoun. "Why should the South be forced to yield?"

The Southerners, led by Calhoun, again threatened to leave the Union if they could not have their way on every measure.

"This time they mean it," Henry Clay said anxiously to one of the senators.

"A slave is like a piece of property," said Calhoun in debate. "Congress has no right to take away a man's property. It is against the Constitution."

"There is a higher law than the Constitution," answered Seward. "That is the law of God which says every man should have his freedom."

Henry was greatly concerned about the problem. "Slavery is the only matter talked about here," he wrote a friend. "I am wondering whether any over-all plan can be proposed that will satisfy all sides."

He had forgotten his intention to do little during this session and to make few speeches. He began to talk about an "over-all" plan with his fellow senators.

"The only way to settle this matter," Henry told them, "is to put all the bills regarding slavery together. Then each side might give in a little, and we would have peace."

Within a very short time, he won Daniel Webster to his side. Webster promised that he would support any bill that Henry Clay proposed.

Early in 1850, Henry read his Compromise Bill in the Senate. California was to be admitted as a free state. This should satisfy the North. To please the South, there was to be a strict law so that fugitive or runaway slaves could be captured easily. There were three other parts in the Compromise Bill in which each side lost a little.

All through the spring and summer, the Compromise was debated in Congress. Day after day, Henry rose to defend his bill. Once he was accused of being a Southerner who had gone against the interests of his own part of the country.

"I know no North — no South — no East

— no West," Henry thundered in reply. "I owe loyalty only to Kentucky and the United States."

On March fourth, Calhoun's views were heard. He was wrapped in blankets and carried into the Senate. Calhoun was so weak that another senator had to read his speech. The only way the Union could be preserved, Calhoun insisted, was to yield completely to the demands of the South. He refused to accept Clay's Compromise Bill except for the part regarding runaway slaves.

Three days later Webster answered Calhoun's speech. "I speak today not as a Massachusetts man, not as a Northern man, but as an American," said Webster. Then he pleaded with the senators to accept the Compromise Bill.

This is the greatest speech Webster has ever made, thought Henry as he listened.

There were shrieks and angry hisses from the gallery when Webster finished his speech. He was from New England, and the Northerners who heard him felt that he had spoken

against them. But the Union was as dear to Daniel Webster as it was to Henry Clay.

On July 9, 1850, President Taylor died; and Millard Fillmore, the Vice President, became President. Fillmore was one of Henry's good friends and admirers and believed in his views. With the President's support, the Compromise Bill of 1850 was soon passed.

By this time, Calhoun had died. "The poor South! What will become of her?" had been his last words.

Late one evening in October, Henry's traveling carriage rolled into Lexington. He had hoped to escape the crowds. But the news that "Mr. Clay's come home!" had spread, and fireworks and bonfires greeted him as the carriage entered Main Street.

There were many speeches, and the crowds cheered heartily. At last, Henry raised his hand for attention.

"I must ask you to excuse me," he said with a smile. "But there is a little woman at Ashland waiting for me, whom I would rather see than any of you."

183

CHAPTER 14

The Strong Staff
Is Broken

Henry sat before the fire in his parlor in the National Hotel in Washington in February, 1852. Ill health had made him resign from the Senate in December. He rarely went out now except for a carriage drive in the afternoon.

Today he was looking at a gold medal that had been presented to him. On one side there was an engraving of his face. On the other was a list of the dates and chief events of his political life. Henry's expression became a little solemn. What other man had done so much for his country and yet had never been elected President?

"I would rather be right than President," he said half aloud. Was that the truth?

Far back into the past he looked. Personal

glory had played only a small part in his early career, he decided. Politics then had been only a game. But later had come his ambition to be President. Sometimes, it had made him forget everything else. Had he ever sacrificed his beliefs in order to be elected?

A slow flush came into his cheeks. He was thinking of the election of 1844. Why hadn't he been honest and said he was against the annexation of Texas? He had been right. It had brought about the war with Mexico. It had added to the number of slave-holding states.

I might have been elected, if I had stuck to my beliefs, he thought.

But how about all the other times in his career when he had lost followers by standing for something that would save the Union? The Missouri Compromise? The Tariff Compromise? The Great Compromise of 1850?

"No North — no South — no East — no West," he repeated softly. "I *would* rather be right." He was comforted by the thought.

186

The days went by. Henry's strength grew less. Even the carriage drives ended. But letters, messages, and gifts poured into his rooms at the National Hotel.

If only I could get back to Ashland, thought Henry.

He longed to see his fields and thoroughbred horses again. But most of all he wanted to be with Lucretia. Each letter he received from her told of her worry and her desire to be with him. But Henry Clay had refused to let any of his family come to Washington. Only his servant Charles was with him. Long ago, Henry had given Charles his freedom, but the Negro had refused to leave his master.

Early in May, Thomas Clay came to be with his father. Thomas was over his wild days now. He was married and had a family. Each day after that, Henry became weaker. On the morning of June twenty-ninth, he was only half conscious.

"My dear wife," he murmured once. "Sweet, sweet Lucretia." He died shortly after eleven o'clock in the morning.

The whole nation mourned the death of Henry Clay. The Senate and House of Representatives were adjourned. It seemed that all of Washington rode or walked to the funeral service at the church. "How is the strong staff broken," was the text of the sermon.

Through black-draped towns, the funeral train took its solemn way. New York City, Buffalo, Cleveland, Columbus, Cincinnati, Louisville, and Frankfort — each had a funeral service. Citizens stood in line for hours and filed slowly by the coffin. Few men in the history of the country had been so honored and so mourned.

At sunset on July ninth, the train reached Lexington. Thousands were gathered there. The buildings and houses were draped in black. Mr. Clay had "come home" for the last time.

By the light of hundreds of torches, the hearse moved along the Richmond Pike to Ashland. An honor guard of horsemen rode before it. Behind it were hundreds of carriages. In the doorway of the house stood Henry's beloved Lucretia and their four sons. Gently the guard of honor carried the coffin into the drawing room.

The last ceremony was at Ashland. Here on the morning of July tenth, the coffin was placed on the terraced lawn outside of the house. The grass was covered with wreaths and flowers. The day was as beautiful and clear as the happy spirit of Henry Clay.

He is buried now in the cemetery in Lexington. A tall shaft of marble is above his grave. On the four sides of his tomb are carved the words, "No North — no South — no East — no West."

This epitaph is the true expression of Henry Clay's political beliefs. Above all, he loved the nation.

Author's Note

Although this biography of Henry Clay is told as a story, it is based on the known facts of his life. Sometimes it is difficult to find actual accounts of a certain part of a person's life. In the case of Henry Clay, I have had to make up some of the incidents about his boyhood.

For example, there is no actual account of Henry's last day at school, but it is very likely that he learned and recited Patrick Henry's speeches in school. Also, no one knows just how George Wythe and Henry Clay first met. But it is true that Henry Clay and Mr. Wythe were devoted to each other, and that Henry became Mr. Wythe's secretary. Henry was chosen for the job of secretary because of his fine penmanship, good manners, and excellent mind. In the Courthouse in Lexington is the will which Henry wrote when he was about seventy. The penmanship is still beautiful and clear.

Henry Clay's devotion to his wife and family are well known. He was proud of his home and keenly interested in the development of his plantation and livestock. If you go to Lexington today, you can visit Ashland which is now open to the public and which is furnished much as it was in Henry Clay's lifetime. The house is in the heart of Lexington today, and the grounds are only about a block square. On the lawn is a bronze plaque stating what Henry Clay did to bring the first pedigreed horses to Kentucky and how he helped make the state famous for its fine horses and race tracks.

There has been much argument as to whether Henry Clay did mean that he would "rather be right than President." In my opinion, it was a true statement. As I have related, Henry Clay sacrificed his political career three times when he proposed compromises to save the nation.

It is no wonder that when a recent committee in the Senate selected the five greatest senators in our history in order to do them special honor, that they placed Henry Clay at the top of the list.

REGINA Z. KELLY

PIPER BOOKS